Tilman E. Pohlhausen

Technology Buyouts

GABLER EDITION WISSENSCHAFT

Tilman E. Pohlhausen

Technology Buyouts

Valuation, Market Screening Application, Opportunities in Europe

With a Foreword by Prof. Dr. Roswitha Meyer

Deutscher Universitäts-Verlag

Bibliografische Information Der Deutschen Bibliothek
Die Deutsche Bibliothek verzeichnet diese Publikation in der Deutschen Nationalbibliografie; detaillierte bibliografische Daten sind im Internet über <http://dnb.ddb.de> abrufbar

1. Auflage Februar 2003

Lektorat: Brigitte Siegel / Nicole Schweitzer

Der Deutsche Universitäts-Verlag ist ein Unternehmen der Fachverlagsgruppe BertelsmannSpringer.
www.duv.de

Umschlaggestaltung: Regine Zimmer, Dipl.-Designerin, Frankfurt/Main
Druck und Buchbinder: Rosch-Buch, Scheßlitz
Gedruckt auf säurefreiem und chlorfrei gebleichtem Papier
Printed in Germany

ISBN 3-8244-7758-0

Foreword

The public market valuation of technology companies throughout the 1990s is probably one of the most interesting phenomena in recent financial history. No sector has generated more enthusiasm among investors, and no sector has created more millionaires, albeit mostly on paper. Once the bubble burst, the correction process was brutal. The price of technology companies dropped by over 70 percent on average, and a significant number of companies went out of business, while others were simply avoided by the investment community.[1]

Tilman Pohlhausen asks a valid question: Did this downturn in valuation lead to some companies being unjustly undervalued, given their past and expected cash flows? If so, he continues, would such companies be suitable for a concept rarely heard of previously for technology companies: a buyout, possibly even financed to a high degree by debt?

The idea is not new. In contrast to Europe, a number of well-financed private equity funds in the United States exclusively target the technology sector for buyouts. What is new, however, is that many more technology companies, because of their lower valuation, could become targets of buyout investors in Europe, as well.

Ultimately, with his analysis of the buyout attractiveness of European technology companies, the author attempts to estimate the validity of this perception. Keeping in mind that the applied model clearly has both practical and theoretical limitations, its findings appear to support the view that buyout opportunities in the technology sector might now exist in Europe. As part of his analysis, the author also provides a Microsoft Excel-based tool to screen markets for companies with certain buyout attractiveness characteristics.

---

1 The NASDAQ composite drop from its all-time high in March 2002 to July 2002 was over 70 percent, while its much smaller German equivalent, NEMAX, lost over 90 percent during the same period.

It is too early to tell whether we can confidently speak of technology buyouts as an established concept. What we can say, however, is that technology companies are increasingly valued in the same manner as companies in any other sector. Today we know that the same rules apply; why, then, should there be no buyouts in technology?

Prof. Dr. Roswitha Meyer
Chair of Decision Sciences
European Business School, Schloss Reichartshausen

Acknowledgments

The following text is entirely based on a master's thesis I wrote in early 2002 while studying at the European Business School, Schloss Reichartshausen, Germany. It was created in a short period of time, and being the first significant textual work of a student it is of course far from perfect. I nevertheless decided to make the thesis available by publishing it, mainly for two reasons: First, when I started exploring the field of technology buyouts, I was stunned by the lack of available public information, be it in form of academic, press, or professional publications. I, personally, would have liked to read any even imperfect thesis about "technology buyouts". The second reason is the encouragement I received during various conversations with banking and private equity professionals. There seems indeed to be an actual interest in this topic – particularly for the European market where technology buyouts have not been given as much attention as they have in the US.

Given the encouragement and support I received, I would like to express my gratitude to those involved with my thesis at various stages. I would not have been able to write about "Technology Buyouts" had not Professor Roswitha Meyer of the European Business School accepted my proposal. I would like to thank her for her support throughout the writing process; I would also like to thank her research assistants Heiko Rhode and Andre Kleinfeld who gave their time and effort when I "tormented" them.

The thesis was written with the support of Dresdner Kleinwort Capital, the private equity group of Dresdner Bank. Thomas Wiegand provided me with crucial guidance and feedback for which I am truly thankful. His understanding of technology markets and equity as well as debt financing was of great value to my conceptual efforts. Additionally, the Technology Group at Dresdner Kleinwort Wasserstein provided me with essential access to their resources. I would like to thank Cornelius Clotten, Rainald Roth, and the whole team for their kind support.

Furthermore, I thank research assistants Hady Farag and Mischa Ritter of the Chair of Investment and Risk Management at the European Business School for their help at some stages, as well as Konstantinos Karamanlis for his diligent text review. Finally, I would like to express my gratitude to Professor Omesh Kini of Georgia State University, who generously provided me with his feedback and advice on some key points of the text.

I appreciate comments and feedback. My email address is t.e.pohlhausen@usa.net.

Tilman E. Pohlhausen

Table of Contents

List of Figures

List of Tables

List of Abbreviations

a	actual
AG	Aktiengesellschaft
AIM	Alternative Investment Market
API	Application Programming Interface
APV	Adjusted Present Value
BIMBO	Buy-in Management Buyout
CapEx	Capital Expenditures
CAPM	Capital Asset Pricing Model
CF	Cash Flow
CFBDR	Cash Flow Before Debt Repayment
CHF	Swiss Francs
CMBOR	Center for Management Buy-out Research
CSFB	Credit Suisse First Boston
CY	Calendar Year
D	Debt
DCF	Discounted Cash Flow
E	Equity
e	estimated
ed.	edition
Ed.	Editor
EASDAQ	European Association of Security Dealers Automated Quotations
EBIT	Earnings before Interest and Tax
EBITDA	Earnings before Interest, Tax, Depreciation and Amortization
EBO	Employee Buyout
ESOP	Employee Share Ownership Plan
EUR	Euro
EV	Enterprise Value
FTSE	Financial Times and London Stock Exchange
GBP	British Pound
HLT	Highly Leveraged Transactions

I/B/E/S	Institutional Brokers Estimate System
IAS	International Accounting Standards
IPO	Initial Public Offering
IRR	Internal Rate of Return
KKR	Kohlberg Kravis Roberts & Co.
LBO	Leveraged Buyout
LMBO	Leveraged Management Buyout
m	million
M&A	Mergers and Acquisitions
MBI	Management Buy-in
MBO	Management Buyout
MC	Market Capitalization
MDAX	Midcap Deutscher Aktien Index
MS	Microsoft
n.a.	not available
NASDAQ	National Association of Security Dealers Automated Quotations
NEMAX	Neuer Markt Index
P2P	Public-to-private
PE	Price Earnings
PEG	Price Earnings to Growth
PLC	Public Limited Company
R&D	Research and Development
S&P	Standards and Poor's
SMAX	Smallcap Aktien Index
SWX	Swiss Exchange
US-GAAP	United States Generally Accepted Accounting Principles
vol.	volume
vs	versus
w/o a.	without author
w/o pg.	without page
w/o pl.	without place

1 Introduction

For many years, buyouts in the technology sector were almost unheard of.[2] Buyout investors as well as commercial lenders, the providers of debt capital essential to many buyouts, avoided the technology sector. Their preferred targets were in mature, stable industries such as food and retailing. Technology, so went the traditional belief among the private equity community, was too volatile, too complicated, not leveragable, without tangible assets, and finally too risky to support buyouts.[3] In short: "LBO [leveraged buyout] firms have viewed the mixing of technology and financial risk as a recipe for disaster."[4]

Although this has been the conventional wisdom, an increasing number of private equity investors have begun to think otherwise over the recent years. For the first time, private equity funds have been raised that exclusively target buyout opportunities in the technology sector. From September 1999 to March 2001, over US$ 8 billion was invested in technology buyout funds, with newcomer firms like Francisco Partners and Silver Lake Partners raising over US$ 2 billion each.[5] The number of technology buyouts increased significantly during the 1990s, from basically zero to 44 in the US and 56 in Europe in the first nine months of 2000, valued at US$ 8.48 billion and EUR 6.28 billion, respectively.[6]

---

2 A buyout can be described as an investor or management led acquisition of a business, often supported by debt financing, in most cases with the goal of generating excess returns by improving and subsequently selling the company again a few years later. The term "buyout" will further be discussed in section 2.1.

3 See: Deb/Kesavan, A not-so-new idea for a not-so-new economy, p. 76; Wright/Burrows/Loihl, Technology sector buyouts, p. 12; Rabinovitz, Leveraged Buyout's strange return, w/o pg.

4 Barry/Dube/Galante, As technology industry matures, firms see buyout opportunities, w/o pg.

5 See: Schack, LBOverload?, p. 28; original data from Institutional Investor. Additional to that figure, established private equity firms also devoted significant amounts of their ordinary funds to this sector. Another source puts the amount raised by "the top ten private tech and telecom equity funds" in 1999 and 2000 to US$ 15 billion, with "a smattering of smaller funds" having raised another US$ 5 billion. Vicente, Private matters, w/o pg.

6 US figures cited from: Vicente, Private matters, w/o pg; original data from: Thomson Financial Securities Data. Silver Lake Partners reported for the same period technology buyouts valued at US$ 18.5 billion. European figures cited from: Wright/Burrows/Loihl, Technology sector buyouts, pp. 12, 13. Original data from: Centre for Management Buy-out Research (CMBOR)/Barclays Private Equity/Deloitte & Touche. It should be noted that

For people like Kenneth Hao, partner at Silver Lake Partners, the world of technology buyouts is a "totally brave new world".[7]

Though these developments can partly be attributed to the general boom in technology investing, in the late 1990s, technology buyout investors believe that there are strong underlying factors driving the general trend. In their opinion, the technology markets have dramatically matured over the last ten years, both in size and nature. More than 1,000 publicly listed technology firms in the US alone, as well as numerous divisions and affiliates of large technology conglomerates such as Siemens, Philips, and Cisco provide a sizeable market for technology buyout investors.[8] These investors point out that many technology companies today have the characteristics of attractive buyout candidates. And in contrast to the supermarket chains or appliance producers bought out in the 1980s, by their nature technology companies possess considerable growth potential. Some investors even feel that the downturn in the public technology markets since March 2000 has provided them with additional opportunities to acquire potentially undervalued firms.[9]

Academics have given little attention to private equity in general, and even less to technology buyouts in particular. That is unfortunate; for there are many questions to ask: Are technology buyouts different from traditional buyouts? How can investors and lenders account for technology-specific risks? What is the impact on valuation? How formidable is the trend towards technology buyouts? And how do regions such as Europe or Asia compare to the US?

The following work aims to focus both on the theoretical and practical aspects of technology buyouts. We will evaluate to what extent they can be regarded as

---

both sources seem to derive their data on different definitions and/or by different means, therefore one should be cautious in comparing the data.

7 Cited according to: Miller, Buyers finding gold in tech wrecks, p. 3.

8 See: Vicente, Private matters, w/o pg.

9 Technology buyout firm Silver Lake notes on its website: "We believe that while market corrections will affect everyone, these corrections represent great long-term opportunities for Silver Lake." Silver Lake Partners (Ed.), Investment philosophy, w/o pg.

traditional buyouts and what the resulting implications are for their valuation. This will lead us to a spreadsheet-based, simplified buyout model whose adjustment to technology buyouts will be discussed. Applying this model, we will estimate the potential buyout return for over 1,600 European growth companies and finally arrive at a preliminary conclusion about the opportunity for technology buyout investing in Europe.[10]

1.1 Theoretical Formulation

Finance theory has developed a number of valuation approaches that can be applied to derive the worth of companies. As buyouts emerged in the 1980s as an institutionalized form of takeover transaction, financial buyers and their advisors began developing sophisticated valuation models in order to value buyout targets, most of which were mature, slow-growing, and predictable businesses. In parallel, with the growth of the technology sector over the 1980s and 1990s, corporate finance began developing valuation approaches in recognition of the special characteristics of technology firms. However, as buyouts of technology companies were hardly existent, these two schools of valuation rarely interacted. Today, buyout and technology valuation still seem distant in both the practical and academic worlds, separated by their origin and application.

However, with the emergence of buyouts in the technology sector, this separation can no longer hold. It becomes of theoretical interest to investigate the underlying drivers, the impact, and the implications of the convergence of these formerly separated fields. The question arises whether general, abstract criteria can be found that distinguish technology buyouts from traditional buyouts, specifically in regard to their valuation. The application of understandings in technology valuation on the buyout world is of particular interest in that context. Should these elaborations produce any results, a practical application of the derived understandings would provide further insight, as well as a verification of the principles and concepts involved. Moreover, when applied to a sufficiently

[10] The Microsoft Excel model developed by the author is available for free download at http://www.connect.to/techbuyouts. The password is "leverage". More information on the model is in section 7.

large sample of technology firms, it would allow us to draw conclusions about the viability of the technology buyout concept.

1.2 Method and Procedures

The thesis begins with a general introduction to the concept of leveraged and management buyouts in relation to their origin in the 1980s. The focus will be on the clarification of terms used in the later parts of this work, as well as on the presentation of the key value factors behind this transaction form. The latter will provide an essential understanding for the subsequent discussions of valuation. Before that, however, we need to clarify the term of a technology company, which will lead us to a working definition of the technology buyout expression. Following this will be an overview of the more recent developments in the technology buyout market, the goal being to identify the drivers behind the emergence of this previously rare transaction form. Among other things, the rationale of such investments will be discussed, as well as the major market participants and current industry trends.

From this descriptive introduction, the subsequent chapters become more analytical in nature and relate to current valuation practices in corporate finance. After a general introduction to buyout valuation, a simplified valuation model for buyouts based on common valuation techniques is presented, each layer representing a corresponding spreadsheet and analyzed for its assumptions and rationale. In the next step, we draw on previously presented understandings about the nature of technology firms. The implications for valuing buyouts of such firms, both in general and in the case of the developed model, will be discussed. Once satisfactory workability of the valuation model for technology buyouts has been assumed, the model will be applied to major European technology indices along with several additional parameters. We finally arrive at a shortlist of companies with exemplary significance for the study question, leading us to a preliminary conclusion about the current level of attractiveness of buyouts in the European technology sector.

2 The Market for Leveraged and Management Buyouts

The following sections discuss the definitions, relevancy, and underlying principles of the buyout concept in an introductory and general form.

2.1 Definitions

"The existing body of literature concerned with the complex of corporate acquisitions in general and buyouts in particular, is characterized by a large degree of confusion over the terminology used."[11] Indeed, literature has produced a variety of ways for expressing related ideas:[12] LBO (Leveraged Buyout), MBO (Management Buyout), MBI (Management Buy-in), LMBO (Leveraged Management Buyout), BIMBO (Buy-in Management Buyout), HLT (Highly Leveraged Transactions) and related terms such as Going Private or EBO (Employee Buyout).[13] Fortunately, the basic idea behind these expressions is rather simple: A buyout refers to an acquisition of a business, be it a public or private legal entity or a part of a larger legal entity, by a specialized investor or investor group and/or management. Typically, the goal of a buyout is to successfully manage the company and find a full or partial exit (cash out) a few years following the acquisition, frequently through an initial public offering or trade sale. The listed terms stand for various flavors of this concept, some being unique while others are interchangeable.[14] The two most important and widely used terms are leveraged buyout (LBO) and management buyout (MBO).

---

11 Leimbach, Transactions in corporate control: An empirical investigation of the nature, determinants and effects of corporate buyouts, p. 7.

12 The challenge already arises with the correct use of "buyout". Parts of the literature prefer the British form "buy-out" (E.g.: Webb, Management buy-outs), whereas US authors predominantly use "buyout" (E.g.: Kaplan, The staying power of leveraged buyouts). In the following, the later version is used.

13 HLT, a term subsequently not further discussed, was introduced by the US banking oversight authorities in 1990 for acquisitions that are financed to a high degree by debt. See: Borio, Banks' involvement in highly leveraged transactions, p. 5. EBO, in most cases structured through an employee ownership plan (ESOP), refers to an acquisition of a business by its employees. See: Bruner, Leveraged ESOPs and corporate restructuring, p. 54.

14 Most academic discussion about the distinctions between LBOs, MBOs and other terminology relates to the degrees of a certain characteristic, be it management involvement, sources of funds or level of debt financing. Agreement has been reached over the main constituents, but the specific distinctions between the terms remains an ongoing discourse.

Although they often come together, LBO and MBO are not synonymous. Whereas a leveraged buyout (LBO) indicates that the acquisition is significantly financed by debt secured by a target's cash flows and assets,[15] management buyout (MBO) signals a considerable involvement, often the lead of management in that transaction.[16] In many buyouts, both factors play a major role, which has led some academics to suggest the term leveraged management buyouts (LMBO).[17] Smaller buyouts especially might be exclusively management led and not financed by debt; in such cases, the use of LBO would be misleading. Similarly, a company could be bought out by an investor group with hardly any management involvement.[18] Speaking of MBO would be inappropriate in that case. Finally, if the target entity is a public company, the buyout results in a going private, meaning the "transformation of a public company into a privately held firm."[19]

For our purpose, a deepened distinction between LBO, MBO and other variants does not appear useful. Rather, we will apply the terms buyout and leveraged buyout (LBO) broadly and in a non-exclusive fashion, relating them to two characteristics: First, a buyout will be understood as always being motivated by a medium term increase in value with an intention of generating returns for financial investors; second, the investors are understood as attempting to structure the buyout with the highest amount of debt financing possible and feasible to reach that goal.[20] Although not theoretically complete, this understanding will sufficiently serve as a working definition.

---

15 E.g. Brealey/Myers define a leveraged buyout as an "acquisition in which (1) a large part of the purchase price is debt-financed and (2) the remaining equity is privately held by a small group of investors." Brealey/Myers, Principles of corporate finance, p. 1067.

16 If the management is brought in externally after the acquisition, the expression management buy-in or MBI is used, whereas BIMBO is a hybrid of a management buyout and buy-in. See: Bannock/Manser, The Penguin International Dictionary of Finance, p. 189.

17 See: Schmid, Leveraged Management Buyout, p. 43; Fox/Marcus, The causes and consequences of Leveraged Management Buyouts, p. 62.

18 A general characteristic for buyouts, however, is that management receives a significant increase in equity and has greater incentive than before in the success of a company.

19 Weston/Siu/Johnson, Takeovers, restructuring & corporate governance, p. 463. Going privates are also referred to as delisting or public-to-private transactions.

20 Therefore, we do not apply the term LBO exclusively to indicate a largely debt-financed buyout.

2.2 History

The idea of buying a company by raising debt on the company's assets and future cash flows while contributing only a small amount of equity is largely a product of the general economic and financial conditions that prevailed during the 1970s and 1980s in the United States. Sustained economic growth, pervasive inflation, regulatory changes in taxation, a new anti-trust climate and an underlying need for restructuring following conglomerate merger waves were factors that provided the ground for the emergence of leveraged buyouts.[21] Pioneer firms such as Kohlberg Kravis Roberts & Co. (KKR) or Forstmann, Little & Co. began raising institutional money and acting as LBO investors,[22] combining their equity with third party debt capital to buy out ever larger firms. By 1988, the buying power of KKR alone, a tiny firm with a few employees, had reached the size of the gross national product of Pakistan.[23] New financing innovations such as below investment grade bonds, so called "junk bonds", allowed financial buyers to acquire the largest corporations with sometimes as little as a few percent equity of the overall acquisition price.[24] The US$ 24.6 billion buyout of the food and tobacco conglomerate RJR Nabisco became a symbol of greed and excess in the 1980s corporate world, and on Wall Street in particular, well reproduced in popular literature.[25] Although public opinion has often looked critical on the buyout concept as a result, various studies suggested an overall positive

---

21 See: Weston/Siu/Johnson, Takeovers, restructuring & corporate governance, pp. 467, 468.

22 Another common term is private equity firms, though this usually includes venture capital and growth investors.

23 See: Burrough/Helyar, Barbarians at the gate, p. 401.

24 Junk bonds, more formally known as high yield bonds, were debt notes with higher than usual interest, but also greater risk of default. Bond trader Michel Millken's firm Drexel Burnham Lambert became the industry leader and financier of many buyouts before it was forced into bankruptcy in 1989. Although the interest rates on high yield bonds are substantially higher, taking into account historic default rates, the effective yield spread over the US 10-year treasury bond from 1978 to 1999 was only 2.88% (arithmetic annual average). See: Altman/Hukkawala/Kishore, Defaults and Returns on High-Yield Bonds: Lessons from 1999 and Outlook for 2000-2002, p. 38.

25 See: Burrough/Helyar, Barbarians at the gate. Other popular books on the Wall Street events and atmosphere of the later 1980s include: Auletta, Greed and glory on Wall Street: The fall of the house of Lehman; Bruck: The predators' ball: The junk-bond raiders and the man who staked them; Steward: Den of the thieves; Lewis: Liar's Poker: Rising through the wreckage on Wall Street; and Partnoy: F.I.A.S.C.O.: Blood in the water on Wall Street.

economic effect resulting from the LBO activity of the 1980s.[26] It is now widely believed that the buyouts of the 1980s brought much needed change in corporate governance and the allocation of economic resources, leading to a significant increase in shareholder value and overall economic competitiveness.[27]

In 1990 and 1991 buyout activity dropped considerably, as new regulations, recession and major corporate defaults had their effects on financial markets. From 1992 on, along with renewed economic growth and reviving debt markets, leveraged buyout activity slowly but continuously picked up. By 1995, the amount of outstanding high yield debt was already greater than that at its previous peak times in the late 1980s.[28] In 1998, over US$ 60 billion of leveraged buyout transactions took place.[29] A new trend was the use of less debt and more equity; over the 1990s, the average equity participation of the overall acquisition price rose from 22% in 1992 to 38% in 2000, as shown in the figure below:

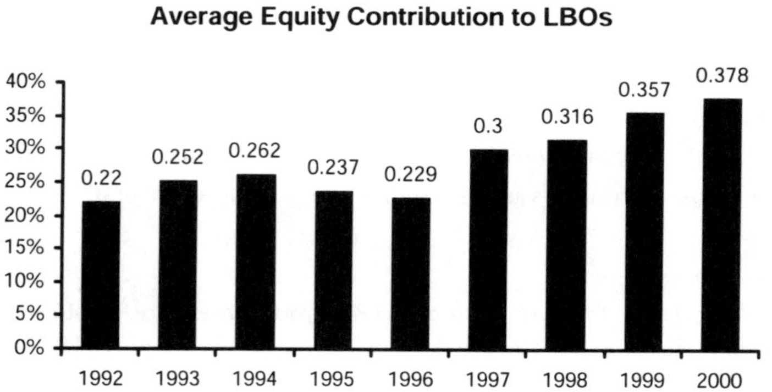

Source: S&P / Portfolio Management Data

Compiled from: RCW Mirus (Ed.), Management buyouts, w/o pg.

Figure 1: Increase in LBO equity contribution

---

26 "The popular media's stories about this [buyout] phenomenon differ markedly from the stories told by careful academic research." Jensen/Chew, US corporate governance: Lessons from the 1980s, p. 337.

27 See: Jensen/Chew, US corporate governance: Lessons from the 1980s, p. 337.

28 See: Weston/Siu/Johnson, Takeovers, restructuring & corporate governance, p. 490.

29 See: Weston/Siu/Johnson, Takeovers, restructuring & corporate governance, p. 465. Original data from: Merges & Acquisitions almanac issues.

Private equity fundraising for buyouts increased dramatically from under US$ 5 billion in 1991 to nearly US$ 55 billion in 1998, with continued growth.[30] Much of the recently raised surplus of LBO funds has not been invested yet, which promises an active buyout market over the next years. Overall, leveraged buyouts appear to have become a "permanent feature" of the financial landscape.[31]

2.2 Value Generation

The average financial performance of leveraged buyouts has historically been very strong, explaining much of their attractiveness to institutional investors. Sampling US LBOs from 1985 to 1994, Anslinger and Copeland concluded that there had been an excess return of 10.7% over the S&P 500 index in the same period.[32] In analysis by research firm Venture Economics, average internal rates of return, the common measure of success in the industry, were found to be over 20% for the first quartile of funds and over 10% for the median in the period from 1987 to 1997.[33]

---

[30] A major driver is the growth in global pension fund assets, of which a few percent are usually invested in so-called alternative investments, with private equity having a major share of that. In their most recent Report on Alternative Investing (December 2001), Frank Russel Company and Goldman Sachs conclude that "investors globally are increasingly looking to private equity to diversify their [asset] allocation and boost return on investment". W/o a., German institutions keen on private equity, w/o pg.

[31] Kester/Luehrman, Rehabilitating the leveraged buyout, p. 119.

[32] Returns cited according to: Weston/Siu/Johnson, Takeovers, restructuring & corporate governance, p. 463. Original data from: Anslinger/Copeland, Growth through acquisitions: A fresh look, pp. 126-135.

[33] It is important to note that rates of return of private equity funds are usually not reported in public and both commercial as well as academic analysis is only based on a sample of funds, which may lead to different results over the same period of time. Most agree though that private equity investing has historically provided higher average returns than public market investing on a risk-adjusted basis.

Internal Rates of Return and Average Transaction Size for Buyouts from 1987 to 1997

Year	87	88	89	90	91	92	93	94	95	96	97	Average
1st Quartile (%)	16.8	14.3	22.3	18.6	21.6	24.1	25.1	30.1	20	38	0	21.0
Median (%)	11.2	11.7	14.5	15.5	14.5	20.8	22.8	15.6	1.7	4.6	-4.9	11.6
4th Quartile (%)	5.9	8.5	8.3	1.3	10	8.5	14.2	2.7	-7.3	-2.2	-23	2.5
Average Size ($ m)	358	272	425	177	83	92	102	142	188	184	233	205

Source: BARRA Rogers Casey; Original Data from: Venture Economics; Compiled from: Haugen, Buyouts as an investment opportunity, pp. 8, 9.

Table 1: Rates of past LBO returns

The sellers benefit even more from LBOs: DeAngelo/DeAngelo/Ricce found an average cumulative return of over 30% for shareholders among 81 firms that went through a buyout.[34] The high rate of return for LBOs clearly leads to the larger question: How can such extraordinary returns be generated? More specifically, what are sources of value in an LBO? Several answers are suggested in the literature:

- **Earnings and sales growth**

  Following a buyout, management usually receives substantial equity ownership and often invests personal money along with financial investors. This leads to increased incentive for the management team to deliver positive operating results. Ultimately, if sales and earnings significantly increase subsequent to a buyout, a company can be fully or partially resold at a high price, leading to substantial financial rewards for the managers involved (as well as high returns for the investors). Edward Gilhuly, managing director at KKR, puts it the following way: "At the very essence of the modern buyout is having management take an ownership stake, providing an incentive to build the business over time."[35]

---

34 See: DeAngelo/DeAngleo/Rice, Going Private: The effects of a change in corporate ownership structure, pp. 43.

35 Gilhuly, Private equity investors in the new European marketplace, p. 77.

Academics have identified two primary effects of such management incentives. Some point to the operating efficiency gains associated with many buyouts,[36] while others stress the entrepreneurial and innovative results.[37]

- **Leverage**

  Through the use of debt, equity investors can increase their expected returns, referred to as leverage effect.[38] Theoretically, as long as the return on assets is above the cost of debt, the expected return of equity can be increased by gearing.[39] Finance theory provides three further reasons for the use of debt in LBOs. The first is an optimization of a company's capital structure, especially for companies that previously had too little debt relative to their optimal debt ratio.[40] The second reason relates to the disciplinary effect of debt on a company's spending of free cash flows; Jensen, among others, has argued that leveraged buyouts lead to a transfer of free cash flows back to shareholders that otherwise would be invested poorly.[41] Third, since debt is to be paid from pre-tax income, a high leverage provides tax shields; these have been identified empirically as another significant source of value.[42]

- **Undervaluation**

  Obviously, buyout investors aim to buy low (i.e., cheap) and sell high.

---

36 See: Kaplan , The effects of management buyouts on operations and value, pp. 217-254.

37 See: Wright, Entrepreneurial growth through privatisation, p. 591.

38 See: Brealey/Meyers, Principles of corporate finance, p. 1065.

39 However, more debt will increase the financial risk of the firm, leading to an offsetting effect on the present value of the investment due to higher costs of capital.

40 In theory, the optimal debt to capital ratio is reached when the benefits of more debt are equally offset by its disadvantages, namely higher financial risk. Economists speak of equal marginal utility and marginal costs of debt. Theoretically, the optimal debt to capital ratio is where the average costs of capital are minimized. An optimization of the capital structure, however, can only explain the use of debt in part, as the debt level in most LBOs exceeds the optimal debt ratio initially. See: Damodaran, Corporate finance, p. 869.

41 "The problem is how to motivate managers to disgorge the cash rather than investing it below the cost of capital or wasting it in organizational inefficiencies." Jensen, Agency costs of free cash flow, corporate finance and takeovers, p. 328.

42 See Kaplan, Management buyouts: Evidence on taxes as a source of value, pp. 611-632.

Sometimes also referred to as multiple arbitrage, the goal is to generate returns through deal-specific differences between the acquisition and exit multiple. Although public and private financial markets have reached a high degree of efficiency since their inception, there are examples of questionable market pricing on which LBO investors attempt to capitalize.[43] The sometimes enormous difference in the valuation of firms in the same industries, as well as the existence of neglected, rarely followed sectors or companies, adds to this situation. To what extent management insider knowledge about the undervaluation plays a role in that context has also been subject to academic discussion; studies indicate that inside information is not a significant source of value.[44]

It is widely believed that the sources of value in LBOs have shifted since the 1980s. Whereas much of the value generated in the early years was perceived to result from financial engineering, specifically via by the amplification of equity stakes in acquisitions through leverage, the contemporary focus has predominantly shifted towards increased operating performance as the major source of value in LBOs. In a survey by Asset Alternatives, buyout limited partnerships estimate that more than 50% of buyout investment return is driven today by company-specific and industry-wide growth in earnings and sales, whereas only a quarter of buyout returns is estimated as a result of leverage (see next figure). Even though capital markets are believed to have gained liquidity and efficiency since the 1980s, undervaluation appears to remain a significant source of value for LBOs.

---

43 Seagate Technologies, a company that went through a buyout in 2000 (as described later on) was trading for less than the value of its marketable securities prior to its buyout. The company has spun off its software division to Veritas Software in a stock deal in May 1999. Following a 200% rise in Veritas' stock price, the equity value of Seagate was less than the market value of its stake in Veritas. Other examples include Palm/3com, where 3com was worth less than its stake in Palm following the Palm IPO, and Fayrewood/ComputerLinks, where Fayrewood is trading for less then the value of its stake in Neuer Markt listed ComputerLinks.

44 See: Kaplan, The effects of management buyouts on operating performance and value, pp. 217-254; Smith, Corporate ownership structure and performance, pp. 143-164.

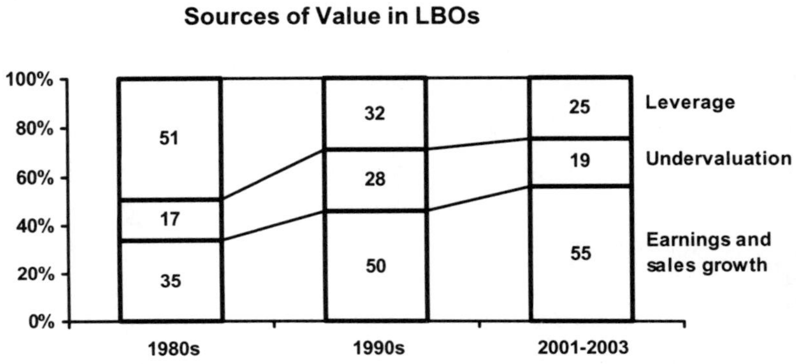

Edited from: Asset Alternatives (Ed..), Strategies for successful buyout investing, w/o pg.

Figure 2: Estimated sources of value in buyouts

In summary of the main value drivers, an attractive buyout target company would have the following characteristics: Low relative valuation, low level of debt, high cash flows to cover interest payments, inside or outside management team with the ability to improve operating performance, and medium-term exit opportunities. It is therefore possible to directly relate the returns achievable in a buyout to a few key factors.

3 The Emergence of Technology Buyouts

Technology firms are often regarded as lacking two of the aforementioned traits that characterize an attractive LBO target: low valuation and high cash flows. To reflect on how technology firms became targets for leveraged buyouts, the following treatment first looks at the meaning of the term "technology firm", and follows up with a discussion of the rationale for technology buyout investing. Some final remarks consider current trends surrounding the "emergence of technology buyouts".[45]

3.1 Definition of a Technology Company

"Technology firms are different."[46] The current literature has in many ways attempted to define this difference and foster a deeper understanding of the attributes of technology firms. Generally, a technology firm's business is regarded as the "linkage between scientific discovery and the delivery of practical results."[47] Innovation and the application of scientific discovery commonly characterize technology firms.[48] Transposing the abstract ideas onto existing companies and industries has proven to be more difficult. Damodaran suggests in his book about the valuation of technology companies a two-sided definition: Technology firms either deliver "technology-based or technology-oriented products", namely hardware and software, or they specifically utilize technology to deliver products or services.[49] The latter definition obviously allows for a broad understanding and depends on the defined degree of technology utilization. In practice, analysts who by profession classify firms

---

45 "Emergence of Technology Buyouts" was originally the title of an unpublished paper written by Taylor at Harvard Business School. Taylor, The emergence of technology buyouts, w/o pg. See: Andrade/Gilson/Pulvino: Seagate Technology Buyout, p. 1.

46 Damodaran, The dark side of valuation, p. XV.

47 Boer, The valuation of technology, p. V.

48 The American Heritage Concise Dictionary defines technology as "the application of science, especially in industry or commerce." Houghton Mifflin Company (Ed.), The American Heritage Concise Dictionary, p. 435.

49 Damodaran, The dark side of valuation, p. 2.

often draw the distinction along industries lines (semiconductor, software, etc.) that are considered to meet the above definitions to a high degree.[50]

Academics furthermore have attempted to identify general characteristics of technology firms for the purposes of categorization. Baruch, for instance, suggests classifying firms as technology companies based on their R&D activity and on the proportion of staff with an academic qualification.[51] Another useful approach, particularly in a finance context, would be to portray the special characteristics of technology companies with respect to risk and return. Commonly, technology firms are seen to inherit risk characteristics that clearly differentiate them from non-technology companies:

- Technology replacement risk (disruptive technologies)[52]
- Product/service development risk[53]
- Short product life cycles
- Employee knowledge dependency
- Earnings volatility[54]

The return of technology firms is driven by growth more so than traditional firms. The US technology industry grew on average four times faster than the rest of the economy from 1988 to 1999.[55] Growth and growth expectations are central to any technology firm. Therefore, instead of industry-linked definitions, a broader understanding is put forward which characterizes a technology firm as

---

50 The difficulty is apparent as information services like Value Line, Morningstar or Bloomberg have different criteria for their industry mappings, with sometimes the same firm categorized differently.

51 A third criteria for the classification as a technology company is that the firm's area of activity is "advanced technology", similar to the definition used by Damodaran. See: Baruch, High technology organization – what it is, and what it isn't, p. 179.

52 Clayton Christensen extensively discusses the nature of technology replacement risk. Christensen, The innovator's dilemma: When new technologies cause great firms to fail.

53 This translates into higher average capital requirements of technology firms.

54 However, Deb/Kesavan note that the volatility of technology firms is only larger in absolute terms, not in relative terms once the higher level of base line growth has been adjusted. See: Deb/Kesavan, A not-so-new idea for a not-so-new economy, p. 75.

55 Cited from: Gallo, Francisco Partners, p. 17. Original data from: US Department of Commerce, Bureau of Economics Analysis.

above all a high growth enterprise.[56] Overall, higher risk and higher (expected) return seem to be financial attributes of the average technology company.

3.1 Investment Rationale

The minimal degree, to which academic literature has covered the field of technology buyouts, be it empirical, analytical, or descriptive, is surprising at first glance. Only a few publications on technology buyouts are to be found. Mainly, the available academic work results from research activities from the Center for Management Buy-out Research (CMBOR) in the UK, course work and case studies related to private equity courses at Harvard Business School, and a few academic contributions in popular media.[57] According to the author's research, the most comprehensive contribution to date was provided by Angela Loihl.[58] In her dissertation on "buyouts in the technology sector" she extensively analyzes three cases of technology buyouts, leading her to the conclusion that "technology buyouts are likely to prevail as a viable investment strategy."[59]

Of the various reasons given for the emergence of technology buyouts in literature and the press, the following appear to indicate the key underlying factors:

---

56 Stressing the growth aspect in technology, Brush for instance notes that "[...] technology, however the definition of technology stretches and shifts to include exotic ventures, is inherently a bet on new, risky activities, often currently unprofitable, but with a high payoff potential. The payoff might never come, but investor expectations, not traditional value, drive prices. A helpful way of thinking about the technology sector is as a category for companies that are using new discoveries. Whether it be railroads, electronic power, radio, television, personal computers, drugs or the Internet makes no difference. As the new technologies mature, the companies move to more staid classifications and eventually become utility-like with limited growth prospects and stock prices determined by current opportunities, not by future growth." Brush, Optimal sector models differ, p.38.

57 Although case studies, published notes or popular press are usually not intended to serve as a primary source of data or information, it was felt that their inclusion in this work would significantly broaden the understanding of the topic, given the limited existence of related information. All sources used have been published, and are marked and listed as such in the reference section.

58 See: Loihl, Buyouts in the technology sector.

59 Loihl, Buyouts in the technology sector, p. 98.

- The technology market has gained critical mass, having grown from a niche segment of the economy to a major economic sector over the past ten years. More than 1,000 public technology companies in the US alone and various private companies and divisions provide a substantial base for buyouts and spin-offs across various market segments.[60]

- An increasing number of companies produce strong recurring cash flows in mature technology areas such as semiconductor, IT-services or software.[61]

- Debt financing became more attainable for technology firms. Deb/Kesavan note that "the debt market is increasingly realizing that many technology companies have excellent credit characteristics".[62]

- The differentiation in public markets technology valuation is substantial. In a sample of 920 US technology companies, the top 15% were valued at a price to sales multiple of 14.9, whereas the bottom 15% were valued at 0.1 times price, indicating the existence of lowly valued firms relative to their performance.[63]

- Because of they are too small or lowly valued to be followed by the mainstream investment community, some technology companies may no longer find the desired financing in public capital markets, whereas private investors might be available in that function.

---

60 McNamee, partner at technology buyout fund Silver Lake Partners explains in an interview: "Ten years ago, there probably wasn't an opportunity, but over the last ten years technology's gone from being this tiny niche to the third-largest sector of the U.S. economy." Lenatti, Targeting tech for leveraged buyouts, w/o pg.

61 See: Deb/Kesavan, A not-so-new idea for a not-so-new economy, p. 76.

62 See: Deb/Kesavan, A not-so-new idea for a not-so-new economy, p. 77.

63 See: Gallo, Francisco partners, p. 19. Original data from Standard and Poors/Compustat/Merrill Lynch, October 1999. Although the overall valuation has substantially decreased since then, the spreads can still be considered substantial, meaning not all technology companies are 'expensive'.

- Wright/Burrows/Loihl point to competition among private equity investors as another factor for the growth in tech buyouts. As competition increased over the recent years, they "have had to seek deals offering increased returns through growth."[64]

- Finally, the impact of the technology bull market from 1998 to 2000 indisputably played a role. Although technology buyouts began before the "New Economy", the general obsession with technology substantially eased the fund raising for this novelty concept.[65]

Even the strongest proponents for buyout investing in the technology sector admit that not all technology companies would suit as targets. For the most part, buyout investors have targeted public companies from out-of-fashion, mature sectors, and corporate divisions that were no longer considered core. The average leverage has been substantially lower than for traditional buyouts, often in the range of 1:1 or less. Needless to say, companies without positive cash flows or a short-term perspective to generate them – not rare in technology – do not qualify as buyout candidates. But, as the technology universe widens, technology buyout investors hope to find an increasing number of targets that meet their criteria. The past record of transactions suggests that they successfully do so, and in opposition to the targets of their traditional buyout colleagues, their investments possess substantial growth potential. In the end, much of the rationale for technology buyout investing can be summarized with a few words: "There's more risk, but on the other hand, there's more growth."[66]

---

64 Wright/Burrows/Loihl, Technology sector buyouts, p. 12.

65 It is therefore no wonder, that the major funds were raised during 1999 and 2000, but not all of them (as shown in table "fundraising activity", section 3.3). With the market downturn, some feel that the timing of those funds was excellent, as they raised in high spirit markets and can now invest in bear market conditions.

66 Quote from Kenneth Hao, partner at Silver Lake Partners. He continues: "If you invest in no-growth businesses and you 're making your gain from leveraging and then deleveraging, at some point, then your marking is very small." But "[...] when you 're looking at 20 percent growth and a longer term approach [...] the reward is potentially much greater." Cited according to: Miller, Buyers finding gold in tech wrecks, p. 3.

3.2 Technology Buyout Investors

The short history of technology buyouts begins with the high-profile failure of Prime Computer in 1989, a minicomputer manufacturer that was saddled with over a US$ 1.3 billion debt at that time.[67] For a long spell afterward, there were no large buyout transactions in technology; that changed in 1996, when LBO firms Texas Pacific Group and Sprout acquired GT Com and Paradyne Networks (formerly part of Lucent Technologies), earning an internal rate on return (IRR) of 49.8% and 110.6%, respectively.[68] Since then, the number of buyouts in the technology sector has steadily increased along with the average transaction size. The table below presents selected high profile technology buyouts and divestures from 1998 to 2002, ranked by value.

Date	Target Name	Target Industry	Seller Name	Acquirer Name	Value (m)
11/22/00	Seagate operat. bus.	Comp. Hardware	Seagate Technology	Investor Group	2,000
07/26/02	Demag Holding	IT Serv./Industrial	Siemens AG	Kohlberg Kravis R.	1,690
05/11/99	On Semiconductor	Semiconductors	Motorola	Texas Pacific Group	1,600
07/12/00	Italtel Spa	Enterprise Soft.	Telecom Italia SpA	Clayton Dubilier & R.	955
03/15/98	Dynatech	Network Com.	P2P	Clayton Dubilier & R.	848
10/01/00	Siemens Nixdorf Inf.	Computer Services	Siemens AG	Consortium	785
12/31/99	CHIPPAC CO	Semiconductors	Hynix Semiconductor	Bain Capital LLC	500
02/01/01	AMI Spinco Inc	Electronic Comp.	Japan Energy Corp	Consortium	420
01/03/01	Tietoenator Oyj	Computer Services	Sonera Oyj	Investor Group	391
07/21/98	Zilog	Semiconductors	P2P	Texas Pacific Group	380
04/08/00	Legerity Inc	Semiconductors	Advanced Micro Dev.	Francisco Partners	375
04/08/00	Information Solutions	Computer Services	Reynolds & Reynolds	Carlyle Group Inc	360
12/24/01	IPC Trading Systems	Transactional Soft.	Global Crossing Ltd	GS led group	360
02/28/99	Telephone switching equipment unit		Daewoo Telecom	Laves Investment Inc	346
09/19/00	OpNext Inc.	Fiber Optics	Hitachi Ltd	Clarity Partners	321
06/30/99	Danka Services Int.	Electronic Forms	Danka Business Sys.	Schroder Ventures	300
05/04/99	Integrated Circuit Sys.	Semiconductors	P2P	Bain Capital LLC	293
09/03/98	Micron Custom Manufacturing		Micron Technology	Cornerstone Equity	271
01/14/01	Ssangyong	Computer Services	Ssangyong Cement	Newbridge Capital	237
11/30/00	IT division	Computer Services	Daewoo Telecom	City Venture Capital	234
07/13/00	Computershare Ltd	Computer Services	Telstra Corp Ltd	Investor Group	226
01/11/99	Asat Holdings Ltd	Electronic Comp.	QPL International	Investor Group	200
06/13/00	SHPS Inc	HR Soft.	SYKES Enterprises	Welsh Carson A.&S.	166

67 See: Gallo, Francisco Partners, p. 5. Smaller, previous buyouts shall be neglected in that context.

68 The stated return figures only represent those of Texas Pacific Group. Source: Gallo, Francisco Partners, p. 13; Original data from: Francisco Partners, L.P. Offering Memorandum. It should be noted that Paradyne Networks was only half realized at the time when the offering memorandum was published, and the current rate of return might be less due to a lower market valuation of Paradyne Networks.

Date	Target Name	Target Industry	Seller Name	Acquirer Name	Value
12/19/01	Leybold Optics	Optical Supplies	Unaxis Holding AG	Investor AB	150
11/14/01	MEMC Electronics	Electronic Comp.	E.ON AG	Texas Pacific Group	138
05/12/01	Hyundai Curitel	Cellular Telecom	Hynix Semiconductor	Consortium	114
07/14/00	SmartStream Sys.	Electronic Payment	Geac Computer	Investor Group	108
05/07/01	Atea	Computer Services	WM-Data AB	3i Group Plc	95
09/11/01	SGI Japan Ltd	Computers Sys.	Silicon Graphics Inc	Consortium	95
01/07/02	Cedar Group	Enterprise Soft.	P2P	Alchemy Partners	68
03/31/02	CSK Electronics Corp	Distribution/Whole.	CSK Corp	Venus Fund Holdings	65
12/20/01	Logic Control SA	Enterprise Soft.	Grupo Picking Pack	Investor Group	63
08/13/01	Legacy business	Applications Soft.	MERANT Plc	Golden Gate/Parallax	62
05/30/01	PSI Technologies	Electronic Comp.	RFM Corp	Merrill Lynch & Co	40
08/06/00	Voice & Data Bus.	Communications	Aztec Technology	Morgenthaler Vent.	35
09/06/98	Viewlogic Systems	Software	Synopsis	Sprout	32
12/11/01	DataDirect Tech.	Computer Services	MERANT Plc	Golden Gate Capital	30
07/08/02	VeriFone Inc	Electronic Payment	Gores Technology	GTCR Golder Rau.	*n/a*

Values in million USD/EUR. GBP converted at 1.6 GPB = 1 USD/EUR
Source: Venture Economics, Bloomberg, Company Websites

Table 2: Technology diverstures and public-to-private transactions 1998-2002

New funds were established to specifically target technology buyouts, often combining expertise in traditional buyout investing with technology or venture capital experience among their founders. The most prominent newly founded firms are Francisco Partners and Silver Lake Partners, each raising over US$ 2 billion for its first fund during 1999 and 2000. The following overview demonstrates the positive fundraising climate for technology buyout funds over the recent years:

Major US technology buyout funds raised (Sept. 1999 until March 2001)

Firm	Date	Amount
Golden Gate Capital	Mar-01	$700 million
Thomas H. Lee Partners	Jun-00	$1.1 billion[*]
Francisco Partners	May-00	$1 billion [**]
Texas Pacific Group	Jan-00	$500 million[***]
Thomas Weisel Partners	Jan-00	$1.3 billion
Silver Lake Partners	Sep-99	$2.2 billion

* Joint venture (75-25) with Putnam Investments, primarily making minority investments.
** Total fund size including previously/subsequently raised technology funds: US$ 2.5 billion
*** Plus option to dedicate up to $1.5 billion to tech deals from TPG's main, $3.5 billion fund, which was raised concurrently.
Source: Institutional Investor, Company Websites.
In parts compiled from: Schack, LBOverload?, p. 28.

Table 3: Fundraising activity

Increasingly, traditional LBO investors attempted to acquire technology expertise and also began investing in technology buyouts, such as KKR's acquisition of interconnect maker Amphenol Corp. in 1997.[69] In 1999, KKR along with Goldman Sachs Capital Partners acquired the banking IT division of former Siemens Nixdorf from German technology conglomerate Siemens AG, marking a major technology buyout in Europe.[70] The line between traditional buyout houses and newcomer technology focused buyout firms seems to be disappearing, as technology firms increasingly become the focus of both.

Maybe the most prominent transaction to date was the buyout of leading disk drive maker Seagate Technologies in 2000. Silver Lake Partners along with Texas Pacific Group structured a complex reverse merger and public-to-private transaction valued at US$ 2 billion.[71] To some industry observers, the Seagate buyout had the characteristics of becoming a "landmark transaction, similar in stature to the RJR Nabisco deal in 1989."[72]

---

69 See: Evans, Leveraged buyout firms go tech, w/o pg. Banks also started to show interest, such Morgan Stanley Private Equity with its commitment of $500 million to a technology buyout joint venture with Convergent Partners in 1999. See: Moriarty, Convergent, MSDW eye buyouts in tech sector, w/o pg.

70 See: Kohlberg Kravis Roberts & Co. (Ed.), Kohlberg Kravis Roberts & Co. L.P. and GS Capital Partners have agreed to acquire Siemens Nixdorf, soon to be re-named "Wincor Nixdorf", w/o pg. The transaction was valued at approx. EUR 800 million. In summer 2002, KKR once more acquired several business lines from Siemens in a transaction valued at EUR 1.7 billion, including the network systems group, an networking enterprise service provider. See: Kohlberg Kravis Roberts & Co. (Ed.), KKR acquires 7 businesses from Siemens AG, w/o pg.

71 See: Andrade/Gilson/Pulvino: Seagate Technology Buyout, p. 2.

72 Andrade/Gilson/Pulvino, Seagate technology buyout, p. 4.

3.2 Current Trends

The public market valuation of technology companies has changed dramatically over the several last years. From its March 2000 high of 5,049, the technology-heavy NASDAQ composite index dropped 73% to 1,344 in July 2002. The fall of the German NEMAX index, Europe's leading growth market index, is unprecedented: From 8,583 in March 2000, it dropped to 582 in July 2002, an incredible 93% loss in 28 months.[73] The charts below give some illustration this development.

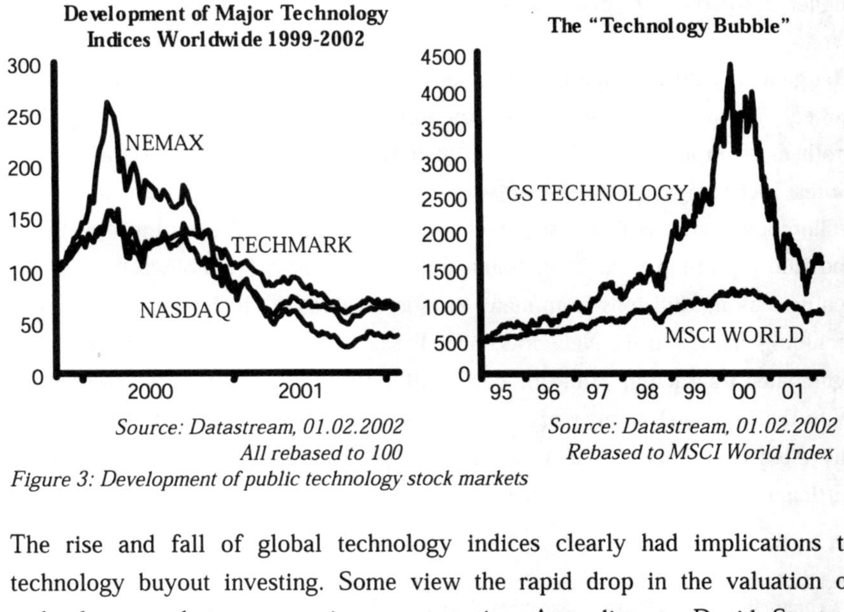

Source: Datastream, 01.02.2002
All rebased to 100

Source: Datastream, 01.02.2002
Rebased to MSCI World Index

Figure 3: Development of public technology stock markets

The rise and fall of global technology indices clearly had implications to technology buyout investing. Some view the rapid drop in the valuation of technology markets as a unique opportunity. According to David Stanton, cofounder of Francisco Partners, "this is the very best time to be an investor".[74] Hao, from rival firm Silver Lake Partners, adds, "There is tremendous opportunity for us to invest in industry leaders that previously were unavailable

---

73 The NEMAX all share index was used. All numbers are rounded. Terminal date for the calculations was July 31, 2002. Source: Websites of NASDAQ and Deutsche Boerse.

74 Statement made at the 13th annual Buyouts Symphosium in New York. Cited according to: Miller, Buyers finding gold in tech wrecks, p. 1.

to us given the craziness in the capital markets".[75] On the other hand, difficult debt markets could disturb this euphoria. With average equity participation as high as 30% to 50% even for traditional buyouts,[76] raising debt for technology buyouts seems even more challenging given the current market conditions: "I haven't seen the financing market [in 2001] this bad in about ten years", says David Dominik, cofounder of technology-focused buyout fund Golden Gate Capital.[77] Spreads for corporate debt have only increased since 2000, and the major corporate defaults of Enron and WorldCom have led investors to flee higher-risk parts of the debt markets.

The generally difficult market conditions have also led to a new trend, or niche, in tech buyout investing: technology turnaround buyouts. Pioneered by two brothers, Tom and Alec Gores, with their firms Platinum Equity Holdings and Gores Technology Group respectively, the strategy here is to acquire distressed technology divisions from large technology corporations, renew their business, and find a profitable exit.[78] Platinum Equity and Gores Technology have so far acquired ailing divisions from many of today's blue-chip technology companies, including IBM, Nortel Networks, and Texas Instruments among others, with aggregated transaction values of US$ 4 billion and US$ 3 billion respectively.[79] With the increased number of corporate defaults in the technology sector, Tom and Alec Gores also began to actively target bankrupt technology businesses, participating in a bidding contest for failed technology brand names such as

---

[75] Cited according to: Miller, Buyers finding gold in tech wrecks, p. 1. Further confirmation comes from Jesse Rogers, managing director of technology-focused buyout firm Golden Gate Capital: "This is an auspicious time for us to start up our operations [...]. With the weak stock market, this year is much better for us than last year would have been." Cited according to: Wade, New equity fund shopping in tech market with $700M, w/o pg.

[76] See: Robb, Acquisition financing in today's volatile marketplace, p.1.

[77] Cited according to: Schack, LBOverload?, p. 28.

[78] See: Lashinsky, Five secrets of a turnaround ace, w/o pg.

[79] Gores Technology speaks of "total transaction value" whereas Platinum Equity quotes "enterprise value" for its number, but specifies not further whether it means the sum of the historic enterprise values at acquisition or a currently estimated one. Other large technology corporations who sold technology divisions to either Platinum Equity Holdings or Gores Technology Group include Williams Communications, Motorola, Staples, Fujitsu, WorldCom, AT&T, CSC, Unisys, Thomson, Mattel, Infinium, Philips, Lucent, Alcatel, and HP. Source: Company websites.

Global Crossing, formerly worth US$ 75 billion. Other private equity investors also seem to be exploring the idea of distressed technology investing, a prominent example being Warren Buffet's Berkshire Hathaway with its investment in Internet carrier Level 3. Much of the rationale of these deals also seems to be the perception of the current market conditions as an opportunity to acquire technology infrastructure built with billions of dollars in the late 1990s at a mere fraction of the original costs.[80] It nevertheless remains to be seen whether the expertise and stronger operational involvement often required for distressed technology investments make them worthwhile for traditional buyout funds.

Both Platinum Equity Holdings and Gores Technology Group have shown little activity in Europe to date, which can be attributed partly to their lacking European presence. There is a strong case that distressed technology opportunities similar to those that exist in the U.S. also exist in Europe, and either these or other specialized investors will be pursuing them.

In general, there is little empirical data available on the quantity and quality of technology buyouts in Europe. According to the buyout database of the Center of Management Buyout Research (CMBOR) of the University of Nottingham, UK, the aggregated transaction values for buyouts in the technology sector have steadily increased since the early 1990s (see next figure).[81] The impact of the change in public market appreciation for technology firms has yet to be seen in these figures, but much speaks for an increased number of buyout transactions, though at much lower valuations.

---

80 As says Level 3 CEO James Crowe who plans to use the investment proceeds for acquisitions: "[The] ongoing shakeout is creating extraordinary opportunities, as telecommunications companies, their network assets and customer bases become available." Bernier, Warren Buffet, Others Invest in Level 3, w/o pg.

81 It should be noted though that the definition used by CMBOR to classify technology buyouts appears to be broader than that of Thomson Financial, possibly overstating the annual transaction values.

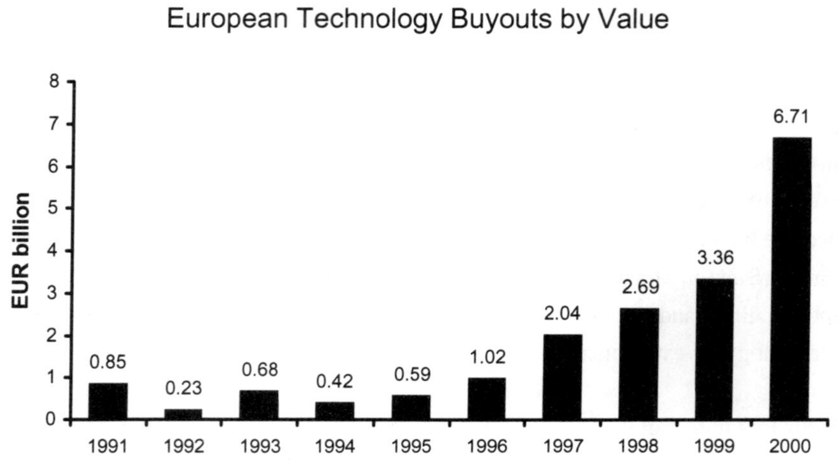

Source: Center for Management Buyout Research/Barclay Private Equity/Deloitte & Touche
Compiled from: Wright/Burrows/Loihl, Technology sector buyouts, pp. 12, 13.
UK figures converted at currency rates as of 7/2/2002: 1.00 GB = 1.625 EUR.
Year 2000 first 9 months only.

Figure 4: European technology buyouts by value

In the end, public technology companies have been much more accessible for private equity investors since 2000, as the acquisition price spent for a company's cash flow has moved to buyout attractive areas.[82] This, as well as the ongoing effort of large European telecommunications and technology corporations to focus on their core businesses (and therefore engage in divestment activities), provides a continuing source of technology related buyout opportunities in Europe.

3.3 Findings and Interpretations

Thus far we have assessed the characteristics of a firm that is an attractive buyout candidate and the objectives of the investors. It is apparent that historically, most technology firms did not fit this description. However, as technology markets have matured and the universe of technology companies has widened, investors

[82] It should also be noted that the offsetting effect on technology buyout investment activity is the at least medium-term limitation in public market exit opportunities. However, investors with a longer-term, value driven approach that is typical for private equity are not discouraged, as recent investment activity has shown.

have increasingly looked at the possibility of buying out technology firms. The number of transactions to date, as well as the substantial commitments made by institutional investors, supports the concept of buying out technology firms as a formidable and existing part of the overall buyout market. We noted that given the outlined characteristics of technology firms, tech buyouts have been structured with less debt and a focus on growth. Apparently, buyout investors hope to offset the greater risk with the prospect of growth. How this can be reflected in buyout valuation will be considered as part of the subsequent chapters.

4 Overview of Leveraged Buyout Valuation

The following passage will provide a brief overview of buyout valuation as a ground upon which to apply a selected valuation approach to technology buyouts. We will, in a very basic form, discuss several valuation approaches, including Weighted Average Cost of Capital, Adjusted Present Value, Changing Cost of Capital, and Equity Cash Flow methods in regards to their suitability for valuing LBOs.

Leveraged buyout valuation is often seen as the high art of financial engineering, since it combines valuing debt and equity in rapidly changing financial structures. There is no single valuation approach that works for every case, and in many transactions buyout professionals use several approaches, all with the aim of providing a clearer picture of whether a buyout is worth pursuing.

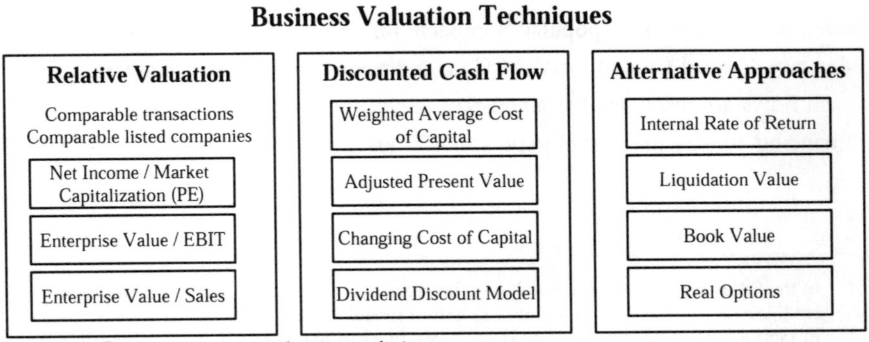

Figure 5: Common business valuation techniques

Practical corporate finance knows two basic approaches to valuing a business, outlined in the above figure along with alternative approaches:[83] Relative valuation based on publicly listed comparable companies or comparable transactions, using multiples such as Price/Earnings or Enterprise Value/EBIT, and fundamental valuation based on the projected cash flows discounted at a rate

[83] The listed valuation techniques do not represent completeness. There are various other techniques or adjustments to the listed approaches, though the above techniques might be regarded as main methods of valuation in today's corporate finance practice.

usually derived from the Capital Asset Pricing Model (CAPM).[84] The latter is a theoretical model developed by Sharpe, Lintner and Mossin, describing the relationship between risk and return of assets, and it thereby provides a way of deriving the costs of equity for business valuation.[85] Even though the CAPM has come under attack from parts of the academic world,[86] it dominates the valuation process, and the understanding of investments and finance in general, as hardly any other theoretical concept.[87] In the average business valuation case, both comparable and discounted cash flow (DCF) analysis are often used in parallel, and assuming fully efficient markets, the market capitalization of a company should at any time equal the discounted value of its future cash flows to equity holders.[88] Therefore, in perfect markets, both comparable and discounted cash flow analysis should yield the same value.

4.1 Weighted Average Cost of Capital Method

A key challenge in discounted cash flow analysis is the derivation of the discount rate. By far the most popular approach for this is the use of the Weighted Average Cost of Capital, or WACC, as a discount rate. WACC suggests that all cash flows are discounted at a constant rate based on the costs of each source of financing, mostly the cost of debt, which is known in many cases, and the cost of

---

84 In the following, we will not touch on other asset pricing models (Arbitrage Pricing Theory etc.), but use the CAPM as the only risk-return model for cost of capital derivation.

85 In fact, it arose from the work of Harry Markowitz in portfolio theory. Twelve years later, William Sharp, John Lintener and Jan Mossin developed a model that essentially suggests pricing assets only according to their market risk as measured by beta, since investors in perfect markets can completely eliminate unique risk through diversification. See: Sharp, Capital asset prices: A theory of market equilibrium, pp. 425-442; Lintener, The valuation of risk assets and the selections of risky investments in stock portfolios and capital budgets, pp. 13-37; Mossin, Equilibrium in a capital asset market, pp. 768-783.

86 Fama and French, among others, have repeatedly pointed to the lack of empirical evidence of a positive relation between average returns and beta, the CAPM proxy for risk. The market risk - return relationship is the fundamental idea of CAPM - and the debate in the academic world continues as to whether a better asset pricing model is in sight. See: Fama/French, The cross section of expected stock returns, pp. 427-466.

87 See: Benninga/Sarig, Corporate finance: A valuation approach, p. 297.

88 If the discounted cash flow value significantly exceeds its market value, the company is undervalued and becomes a takeover target.

equity, which is derived from the CAPM.[89] However, this brings along a major shortcoming, which makes it unsuitable for leveraged buyout situations: The application of WACC assumes a constant financial structure of the company and it therefore does not take into account the financial effects resulting from changing debt loads. As companies going through a leveraged buyout typically take on significant amounts of debt at the time of the transaction and then reduce their leverage drastically, WACC as the most commonly used discount method in finance is not a good choice for leveraged buyout valuation.

4.2 Adjusted Present Value Method

Even before WACC became the de-facto standard, another approach for cash flow valuation known as the Adjusted Present Value (APV) method was formulated by Myers.[90] Although practitioners often refer to it as too academic and complicated, the basic principle of this method is in fact straightforward. Under the APV approach, a company is valued in the first step as if it were financed only by equity; in a second step, the effects of the real financial structure are added to, or subtracted from, this value. To value the positive effects of debt financing, the tax shields are projected for each year and then discounted to the present value.[91] Other tax saving items, such as net operating losses which can be carried forward depending on tax regulation, are valued accordingly.

However, debt also carries costs that reduce the value of the firm as the debt level increases. Theoretically correct use of APV, costs of financial distress, which can be broken down into bankruptcy costs and costs of financial distress

89 For a theoretical derivation of the WACC formula see: Miles/Ezzel, The weighted average cost of capital, perfect capital markets, and project life: A clarification, pp. 719-730.

90 See: Myers, Interactions of corporate financing and investment decisions – implications for capital budgeting, pp. 1-25.

91 The appropriate discount rate for tax shields is still being discussed among academics. In the end though, it has to reflect fairly the risk of its actual realization. See: Loeffler, Tax shields in an LBO, p. 3. Lerner adds that "by convention, the discount rate often used to calculate the net present value of the tax benefits is the pretax rate of return on debt". Lerner, Venture capital and private equity: A casebook, p. 182.

short of bankruptcy,[92] have to be subtracted from the firm's present value weighted by the probability of financial distress. Given the complexities in valuing financial distress, though, this is in practice often neglected and may be interpreted as a shortcoming of the APV method.

To have APV accommodate to the fast changing financial structure of an LBO, the effects of the financial structure are projected for each year using changing leverage ratios according to the debt repayment schedule. The separation of firm performance and effects of financial structure provides a useful approach to LBO valuation.[93] Indeed, empirical tests indicate that the APV analysis provides an overall better fit with observed prices in LBO situations than does the WACC approach.[94]

4.3 Changing Costs of Capital Method

A technically sophisticated approach for LBO valuation is the Changing Costs of Capital method. It is similar to the WACC approach, but instead of using a constant discount rate reflecting the target capital structure, the costs of capital are adjusted for each period according to the firm's leverage, as projected in the debt schedule. The levered beta of the equity and the debt beta are changing as the debt level is reduced over the buyout horizon, and therefore each cash flow period is discounted with decreasing costs of capital. The Changing Costs of Capital method is a precise approach for LBO valuation, but its application is complex and data and assumption intensive.[95] Another drawback of the Changing

---

92 The latter are mostly agency costs of firms in financial distress and monitoring costs of debt holders. See: Brealey/Myers: Principles of corporate finance, p. 528. In an extensive empirical study Andrade/Kaplan estimated the costs of financial distress to be less than 10% of the firm value. Their findings suggest that costs of financial distress are in many cases lower than originally expected and have positive operational effects. See: Andrade/Kaplan, How costly is financial distress? Evidence from highly leveraged transactions that became distressed, p. 24.

93 Similarly, Inselbag/Kaufold conclude in their early paper on LBO valuation that the "APV is ideally suited for LBO applications". Inselbag/Kaufold, How to value recapitalizations and leveraged buyouts, p. 88.

94 Kaplan/Ruback: The valuation of cash flow forecasts: An empirical analysis, pp. 1059-1094.

95 According to Kaufold/Inselbag, the Changing Cost of Capital method is "complicated and rarely done properly". Kaufold/Inselbag, Valuation approaches to the LBO, p. 25.

Cost of Capital method that applies also to the WACC is its exposure to circularity, since the cost of capital depends on the financial structure, and the financial structure depends on the costs of capital.[96]

4.4 Equity Cash Flow Method and Internal Rate of Return

A basic proposition of finance theory is that the enterprise value of a firm equals its value of debt and its value of equity.[97] All approaches so far considered value the firm as a whole. Subtracting the value of debt from the enterprise value then derives the value of equity. However, it is also possible to directly value the equity using the Equity Cash Flow method. Furthermore, instead of using discount rates derived from CAPM, another option is to use an annually compounded return rate to investors, called the internal rate of return (IRR). As we will see, this makes particular sense in LBO situations.

In many buyouts, equity investors have only two cash events. The first cash event occurs when investors pay to acquire the company, while the second (hopefully) takes place when the company is sold to a trade buyer or in an initial public offering.[98] During the time of the investment, all cash generated by the company is typically used to pay down the debt, also called "cash sweep". During this time no cash is allowed to reach equity holders until all debt has been paid off or has been reduced to the target level.[99] The following figure assumes a five-year investment horizon and illustrates the equity investor's cash flows:

---

96 One way to circumvent circularity is to use book values rather than the estimated market values in calculating debt-equity ratios. However, while this might provide an appealing solution in some cases, it will barely work for companies whose equity market value would hardly be reflected by its book value. Also see: Damodaran, Corporate finance, p. 871; Ross/Westerfield/Jordan, Corporate finance, p. 498.

97 See: Miller/Modigliani, Dividend policy, growth, and the valuation of shares?, pp. 411-433.

98 Minimum holding periods following initial public offerings or other contractual extension of ownership shall be neglected. Furthermore, as discussed, other forms of exits are possible.

99 This is usually part of LBO debt contracts. See: Baldwin, Technical note on LBO valuation (A), p. 2.

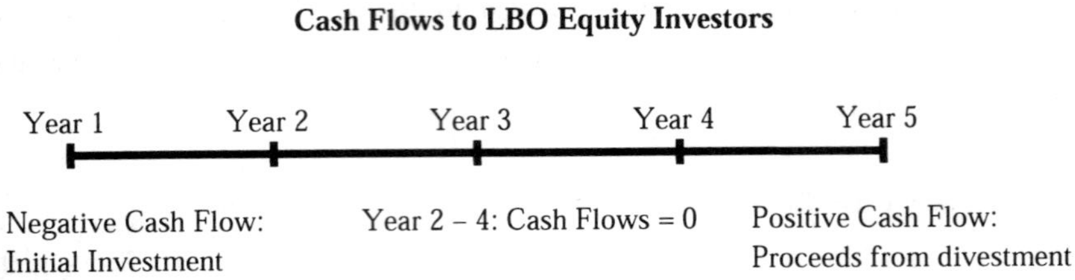

Figure 6: Equity cash flows in a typical buyout[100]

Given the cash flow patterns to investors in buyouts – one outgoing cash flow at the time of the investment and one incoming in the future – the equity cash flow method has special appeal in reflecting this simplicity. Another argument for the Equity Cash Flow method is that it can be easily combined with the target internal rate of return concept described subsequently.

How can we translate the future cash flow of the exit event into a present value? Typically, we would use some form of discount rate that reflects the risk associated with that cash flow. According to finance theory, this discount rate should be determined by operational risk, usually measured through a company's unlevered beta by drawing on the CAPM framework, and financial risk, which depends on the financial structure of the company.[101] Determining a discount rate is already challenging in general, as the effective unlevered cost of equity can be hard to establish, especially in highly volatile public markets and for private companies with no fitting comparables. LBOs carry the added complexity of a rapidly changing financial structure, which will result in varying financial risk over the life of the buyout.

Instead of using a discount rate derived from CAPM and adjusted for the financial structure, another approach suitable for LBOs is to use a target internal

---

[100] See: Baldwin, Technical note on LBO valuation (A), p. 5.

[101] To be precise, only the risk premium part of the discount rate, i.e. the portion above the risk-free rate, is determined by these factors. Naturally, the third determinant for the overall discount rate is the risk-free rate.

rate of return (IRR) to discount the exit cash flow.[102] This target rate, which is the rate of return on an investment when the net present value is zero, is set by the equity investor and has in practice two determinants:

- A minimum acceptable rate of return as set by the buyout fund, often in the range of 25% to 35%, depending on market conditions and the investment strategy of the fund.[103]
- The perceived risk of the particular investment (both operational and financial).[104]

Using a target rate of return, we in effect "outsource" the derivation of a discount rate to the equity investor. By making the discount rate an exogenous variable, the target IRR method assumes that the investor is able to identify his or her discount rate given the above determinants. The positive side effect of this valuation approach geared toward LBOs is that it is substantially less complex and free from heavy-handed assumptions about betas and changing (market valued) capital structures within the calculation.

In fact, using an exogenous target IRR can also be understood as relying on CAPM, albeit indirectly. As with any assets, investments in buyouts (or on an aggregated basis, in buyout funds) carry certain risk and return characteristics. Institutional investors who provide buyout funds with the money to invest arrive at their required return rate by analyzing where these investments lie compared to other assets in their asset pricing model. They find that buyout investments have a high market sensitivity, the CAPM proxy for risk, or high values in risk proxies of other asset pricing models. Therefore, institutional investors require a corresponding rate of return so that there is no other investment with a higher

---

102 See: Baldwin, Technical note on LBO valuation (A), p. 6.

103 The target return of the fund is disclosed to fund investors in the marketing process and serves as performance benchmark.

104 Lerner describes the IRR as the "the yield the [investor] [...] feels is required to justify the risk and effort of the particular investment." Lerner, Venture capital and private equity: A casebook, p. 188. As it will later on be discussed, discount rates imposed on individual projects are nevertheless being seen as problematic among academics. See section 6.1.1.

return at the same level of risk available to them. In the end, the application of the internal rate of return can be seen as an attempt not to circumvent asset pricing models conceptually, but to avoid some of the complexities involved.

Calculating a present value by discounting the buyout exit cash flow using a target IRR, the investor can identify the maximum amount that he or she should pay to achieve a target level of return:

maximum to be paid for target company =
exit equity cash flow / (1+ required IRR)^(cash-out horizon)

Just as we can calculate the present value of a future cash flow given a target rate of return, we can reverse this simple, three-variable equation and solve for the IRR by assuming a known price to be paid for the target company. If this acquisition price is known, and if we can project a future exit cash flow following the buyout, the expected IRR can easily be calculated:

expected IRR = (exit equity cash flow / acquisition price) ^ (1/cash-out horizon) – 1

This simple relationship is the basis of the subsequent model. It should be noted that the expected IRR is not risk-adjusted and should therefore be benchmarked against a hurdle rate or required IRR set by the investor for the specific investment. The subsequently laid-out model will not establish hurdle rates but only offer an expected IRR as an outcome. This, however, is no shortcoming in a relative and preliminary evaluation of investment opportunities, if the expected IRRs were estimated by using similar operational and financial risk assumptions for all companies analyzed. Furthermore, independent of the investment specific risk, buyout investors will only pursue typical buyout opportunities above a certain minimum rate of return. Therefore, estimating an expected IRR provides theoretically sound, but naturally only preliminary information on the degree of buyout attractiveness.

Overall, since a target company is only valued from the LBO investor's perspective, and because of the special cash flow patterns of an LBO, the Equity Cash Flow method with IRR as the discount rate provides an elegant approach to leveraged buyout valuation. It is simpler than the previously discussed alternatives and is indeed "most commonly used in [LBO valuation] practice".[105] Most importantly, it delivers acceptable results close to those achieved when a CAPM-based model with changing capital costs is used, but without the complications involved. "The validity of the target IRR method rests on the fact that it is a good approximation of the Changing Cost of Capital method, which is consistent with finance theory."[106] An interesting feature of the Equity Cash Flow method using target IRRs is the possibility of reversing the approach to estimate expected IRRs. Even without establishing hurdle rates, it allows for a useful first return analysis of investments with comparable risks when the acquisition price is known.

---

105 Baldwin, Technical note on LBO valuation (A), p. 5.
106 Baldwin, Technical note on LBO valuation (A), p. 5.

5 Simplified Valuation Model

Based on the previously illustrated Equity Cash Flow method with a target IRR as a discount rate, we will develop a standardized approach for a preliminary LBO attractiveness evaluation in the following. The result should be a spreadsheet valuation model that can be applied to almost any company and – within the assumptions made – will provide workable indications of the return achievable in a leveraged buyout transaction. Once the model has been established in a general way, we will discuss possible adjustments for technology buyouts and finally employ the model upon publicly available data from European technology markets.[107]

As we have seen, the financial evaluation of buyouts by estimating an IRR, given acquisition value and projected future value of the investment, is both intuitive and appealing. In summary, we can support an application of this concept for a buyout model, because:

- Its results are theoretically sound.
- Its outcome, the IRR, serves as a common measure both for the fund and for fund investors.
- It is significantly simpler to apply than WACC, Changing WACC or APV.

Based on our conviction of the quality of the Equity Cash Flow and IRR approach, we will now apply this method in a general buyout model. The goal is to develop a model that requires as input only publicly available market and financial statement data of listed companies and provides as output only one numerical indicator for the return potential. As we saw in the simple equity cash flow analysis, there are three parameters in the final return calculation of the Equity Cash Flow method: The outgoing cash flow at the time of the acquisition,

---

[107] The Microsoft Excel model that has been developed as part of this publication is available for download at http://www.connect.to/techbuyouts. The password is "leverage". Tables and figures listed subsequently refer to worksheets in the spreadsheet model.

the incoming cash flow at the exit event, and the internal rate of return, which measures the annually discounted return. Since the equity value for listed companies is known, and therefore the approximate acquisition price is also known, we only need to develop a working projection of the exit proceeds to solve for the IRR, our return indicator.

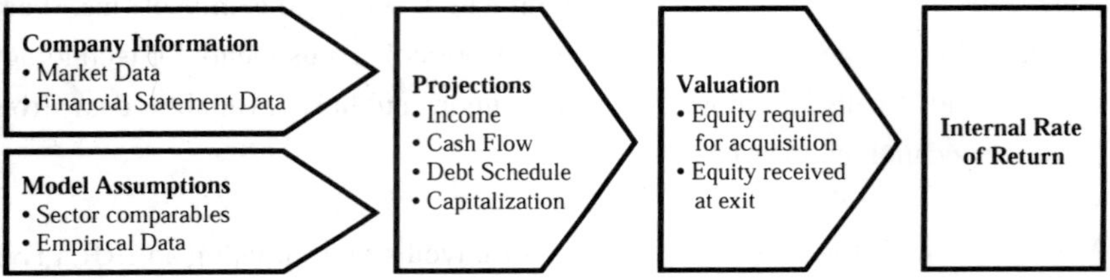

Figure 7: Model overview

The above graph outlines the workings of the model, which can be grouped in four sections, each representing a different spreadsheet in Excel and accomplishing different goals:

- Inputs & Assumptions: Deriving model drivers from various sources
  (Spreadsheet name: InputsLBO)
- Leverage: Estimating debt capacity and cost of debt
  (Spreadsheet name: LeverageLBO)
- Projections: Forecasting the firm's financial statements over the buyout horizon
  (Spreadsheet name: ProjectionsLBO)
- Valuation: Valuing the equity of investors at the time of acquisition and exit
  (Spreadsheet name: ValuationLBO)

Subsequently, the workings of each section will be described.

5.1 Inputs

On the surface, financial models often look frightening. Pro-forma models projecting future cash flows usually consist of complex spreadsheets and include such a degree of detail that readers may be unduly impressed by the precision and forecasting ability of the financial analyst. However, most models can be broken down into a very few and often simple model drivers that impel the model's development over time. These drivers make or break a model, and their rational derivation is a crucial part of any model. We can classify the drivers of the model in two ways: As inputs, which change every time the model is applied to a new target (e.g., market value of a company), and assumptions, which we will assume to be constant for all targets (e.g., net capital expenditures / sales growth ratio). To apply the Equity Cash Flow method in our model and determine an IRR, various inputs and assumptions are required.

First, we need basic financial statement data about the target company, as well as its current market valuation. Therefore, the model requires the following inputs as highlighted in the subsequent figure, "Inputs & Assumptions": Value of cash and marketable securities, value of outstanding debt, market capitalization, current EBIT, current sales and current enterprise value.[108] These inputs required for each target company are marked as "IN" in the table.

[108] The enterprise value will later be part of more detailed discussion. Although cash and market capitalization are known and the enterprise value could directly be calculated this way, it is required as an extra input to account for minority interest.

LBO		
Cash-out Horizon in years	AS	5
Base year (0)	AS	2001
Management Participation (%)	AS	8%
Management Discount (%)	AS	40%
Required cash on hand in % of sales	AS	4%
Cash Account 2001	IN	154.57
Proceeds from Asset Sale	AS	0.00

Income Statement		
Sales 2001	IN	416.63
EBIT 2001	IN	113.76
EBIT 2001 Margin		27%
Average sales growth	AS	15%
Sales growth rate of excess cash	AS	200%
Corporate tax rate	AS	34%
Net CapEx / sales growth	AS	25%
Increase in NWC / sales growth	AS	8%

Debt		
Pre-acquisition Debt	IN	3.26
Long-term bond rate	AS	0.050
EBIT Coverage Ratio 2002	AS	3.5
Rating		BBB
Maximum interest expense		37.4
Cost of Debt		0.0725
Debt Capacity		515.6
Pre-acquisition Net-Debt		(151.31)

Acquisition		
Market Capitalization	IN	791.68
Transaction Costs / Acq. Price	AS	3%
Amortization of Transaction Costs in yrs	AS	5
Acquisition Premium	AS	25%
Minimum equity in % of acquisition price	AS	10%
Exit EV/EBIT if EV at base year < 0	AS	5.00

Multiples (current market)		
Enterprise Value	IN	754.20
EV/EBIT		6.63
EV/Sales		1.81
Exit P/E		13.22

Acquisition Multiples (incl. premium)	
Enterprise Value	952.12
EV/EBIT	8.37
EV/Sales	2.29

Figure 8: Inputs & assumptions (data from Software AG)

Additional to fundamental company data we have to draw on a set of assumptions to realistically emulate the cash flows in a buyout. Many of these assumptions are ratios, allowing the model to derive values from information that we already have. Although different for each company in reality, they are assumed to be the same and constant, which again suits the goal to analyze many companies with the same model. All assumptions required for the model are marked as "AS" in the above figure. The value for each assumption is derived either from empirical evidence based on averages in selected markets that were screened for that purpose, or available estimations from literature or industry practice. While some assumption values apply to buyouts in almost every sector, others are already made specifically with the technology sector in mind. The specific assumptions are listed in the following table:

Assumption	Value	Rationale
Cash-out Horizon in years	5	Five years is being considered a conservative estimate for the average holding period in buyout transactions.[109]
Management Participation (%)	8%	Clearly, management participation depends on deal size and one could make it a function of this. However, an 8% average can be regarded as acceptable approximation.
Management Discount (%)	40%	The discount at which management can buy into a deal varies greatly. 40% less per share than the LBO investor is a reasonable estimation.
Required cash on hand in % of sales	4%	The current ratio of cash in percent of sales among the sample companies is 0.3985 (outliers excluded).[110]
Proceeds from Asset Sale	0	Since there is no possibility to estimate proceeds from potential asset sale following buyouts without individually analyzing companies, it is assumed there will be no proceeds from asset sales.
Long-term government bond rate	5%	Clearly, this is not the exact rate at any given point in time, but should serve as a sufficient proxy. Since the model will focus on European companies, the 10-year Bund rate is chosen as the benchmark.
EBIT Coverage Ratio	3.5	A times interest earned ratio below 3.5 would for many technology firms mean a below investment grade rating. Furthermore, for some technology companies this might already be the bottom limit of what credit providers would accept.
Sales growth rate of excess cash	200%	This assumes that investments from excess cash during the buyout horizon lead to a sales increase of twice the invested amount and is therefore conservatively below the capital expenditures / sales growth ratio.
Average sales growth	15%	Although sales of technology companies have increased at significantly higher rates historically, given today's low visibility and the conservative nature of the model, 15% seems reasonable.[111]

109 See: Richerstein, Buyout, p. 188; Baldwin, Technical note on LBO valuation (A), p. 5.

110 Arithmetic average of the 1,600 plus companies in the dataset, outliers excluded.

111 Another factors contributing to the 15% annual sales growth assumption is the focus of buyouts on technology firms at the lower end of the growth curve.

Assumption	Value	Rationale
Corporate tax rate	34%	Assumed as the average EU corporate tax rate.
Net Capital Expenditures / sales growth	25%	In line with a Damodaran dataset for technology companies, this figure estimates that for EUR 400 of sales growth, EUR 100 have been invested.[112]
Increase in Net Working Capital / sales growth	8%	Since technology companies operate across various value chains with different requirements in net working capital, this average can serve as a sufficient proxy.
Transaction Costs / Acquisition Price	3%	This number is in line with most historical transaction costs for financial, legal and accounting services.[113]
Amortization of Transaction Costs in years	5	Because a five-year buyout horizon has been chosen, the amortization is distributed over the same amount of time.
Acquisition Premium	25%	The current average premium for EU targets is at 10%-15%.[114] To be conservative though, the long-term average premium has been chosen. In addition, there is upward bias in that number due to exclusion of negative premiums as well as the wide range caused by few very large observations.[115]
Minimum equity in % of acquisition price	10%	Even in the roaring late 1980s, equity contribution to target capitalization was not significantly below 10%.[116]
Exit EV/EBIT if EV at base year < 0	5	An EV/EBIT multiple of 5 is significantly below the technology industry average and can be seen as a very conservative exit multiple for this special case.[117]

Table 4: Model assumptions

[112] Technology sectors in dataset on capital expenditures (capex.xls), Damodaran, The dark side of valuation, p. 133.

[113] The current (February 15, 2002) nine months rolling advisory fee to deal size ratio is 1.56% for transactions below US$ 5 billion. Source: Dealogic. See: The Deal (Ed.): M&A acquirer advisory fees - February 21, 2002, w/o pg. Due to usually higher financial, legal and accounting advisory needs in buyout transactions, this number has been adjusted upwards.

[114] Source: Dealogic. See: The Deal (Ed.): Average premiums: European targets – February 7, 2002, w/o pg. The long-term median premium for LBOs from 1993-1998 was 24.2%. Source: Mergerstat Review 1999; compiled from: Weston/Siu/Johnson, Takeovers, restructuring & corporate governance, p. 465.

[115] See: Pratt, Business Valuation: Discounts and Premiums, p. 59.

[116] See: Gallo, Francisco Partners, p. 14.

[117] The EV/EBIT average of the sample company set was 17.83 (06.02.2002). Since companies with negative EBITs were excluded, this number is overstated. An EV/EBIT of 5 can be assumed as conservative minimum.

A general description of the meaning of each assumption and its function in the model can be found in the Field Description Sheet in appendix A. Some of the assumptions relate to special cases to which the model accommodates and are described later in section 5.5. Equipped with working assumptions and the necessary company data, we can now proceed to looking at how the model develops towards the IRR.

5.2 Leverage

As previously discussed, a fundamental concept driving traditional buyouts is leverage. Financing the buyout to the largest possible extent with debt secured by the target's assets and cash flows will increase the return of equity investors.[118] How much debt is a company able to raise or assume, and at what costs? In practice, the dominant criteria is the target's credit rating, which reflects the risk of default on its outstanding debt. Rating agencies such as Standard & Poor's or Moody's assign their ratings by looking at five major factors, which determine the credit quality of a company (ranked by importance):

- Coverage ratios (EBIT and fixed)
- Leverage ratio (book and market value)
- Liquidity ratios (quick and current)
- Profitability (mostly return on assets)
- Cash-flow-to-debt ratio[119]

The rating and the existing conditions in the credit market determine a company's cost of debt. To maintain a certain rating, the company's ratios must stay within the range of its rating class. For example, if a company aims for a AA rating by Standard & Poor, it can on average only raise debt up to the point where its EBIT interest coverage ratio (EBIT/interest) is higher than about 9.5.[120] If the company were to raise more debt, its resulting lower coverage ratio would

---

[118] While it increases the equity risk (beta lever up) as addressed in section 2.3.

[119] See: Bodie/Kane/Marcus: Investments, p. 409.

[120] The number is being taken from an interest coverage ratio table that will subsequently be introduced (Table 5: Synthetic rating estimation).

lead to a rating downgrade reflecting the higher credit risk for lenders. Obviously, the lower the rating, the more costly becomes debt financing. Furthermore, below investment grade debt (BB and lower in Standard & Poor's rating system) is not always available and the amounts that can be raised are significantly smaller.[121] In the mid and late 1980s, when high-yield debt was excessively in supply and historic corporate defaults were low, corporate spreads (the difference between the interest of corporate bonds and government bonds) narrowed across all ratings, and non-investment grade ratings were common for leveraged buyouts. Today, however, given the higher costs of below-investment grade financing and potential difficulties in accessing follow-on financing, there is good reason for choosing BBB or higher ratings. Eventually, this has to be weighted against the potential reduction in equity holder returns.[122]

Assuming management and investors have defined a desired post-buyout rating, how can we derive the debt capacity and costs of debt for the model? A simple way is to reverse a common debt valuation technique for estimating the cost of debt for firms that are not rated. This is referred to as synthetic rating and essentially means to give a company a rating based on its financial ratios and empirical data, linking ratio ranges to ratings. The table below links EBIT interest coverage ratios (EBIT/interest expense) to ratings, and ratings to cost of debt spreads.

---

[121] Especially in Europe where the high yield market is still in an early stage compared to the US, the availability of high yield and mezzanine financing for large transactions is limited. Additionally, many institutional fixed income investors are not allowed to invest in below investment-grade debt.

[122] Compare to the credit rating of Seagate Technologies as discussed in: Andrade/Gilson/Pulvino, Seagate Technology Buyout, p. 8.

Interest Coverage Ratio Table

If interest coverage ratio is			
greater than	smaller to	Rating is	Spread is
-100000	0.499999	D	14.00%
0.5	0.799999	C	12.70%
0.8	1.249999	CC	11.50%
1.25	1.499999	CCC	10.00%
1.5	1.999999	B-	8.00%
2	2.499999	B	6.50%
2.5	2.999999	B+	4.75%
3	3.499999	BB	3.50%
3.5	4.499999	BBB	2.25%
4.5	5.999999	A-	2.00%
6	7.499999	A	1.80%
7.5	9.499999	A+	1.50%
9.5	12.499999	AA	1.00%
12.5	100000	AAA	0.75%

Table 5: Synthetic rating estimation[123]

Reversing the synthetic rating process for the model, we are not looking to estimate the coverage ratio and subsequently the rating; quite the opposite; we assume a fixed minimum coverage ratio based on our desired rating and look for the maximum interest expense that can be paid given this ratio. The formula is:

EBIT / coverage ratio = interest expense

We then know the maximum interest amount that can be paid based on the most recent EBIT and a coverage ratio reflecting our desired rating. In a next step, we estimate how much debt a company can hold with the specified maximum interest expense. Since we can derive the cost of debt from our desired rating by looking up average corporate spreads from the presented synthetic rating estimation table, we are able to calculate how much debt can be supported:

---

123 For companies with less than US$ 2 billion market capitalization. Source: Damodaran Online, Updated data, http://www.stern.nyu.edu/~adamodar/New_Home_Page/datafile/ratings.htm, access date: 3.2.2002. In line with S&P three-year medians 1997-1999, S&P credit week, 09/2000. Updated spreads can be obtained from www.bondsonline.com, Corporate Spreads, by using the Bridge Fixed Income Database for S&P and Moody's rated bonds.

(100 / average cost of debt) * interest expense = debt capacity

Without explicit mentioning, we have not distinguished the different layers of debt, also known as 'tranches' that are usually existent in leveraged buyouts, from senior secured debt to unsecured high-yield and mezzanine debt. This, however, is no shortcoming, since the average cost of debt that we used in the formula is nothing but the interest rate of each layer weighted by its amount of debt. The resulting overall debt capacity therefore is the added amount of debt of all layers. Once we know the debt capacity, we are positioned to calculate how much debt can be raised to finance the buyout:

debt capacity - assumed (pre-acquisition) debt = new debt

So far, we have only looked at one ratio to estimate the debt capacity of a firm: The EBIT interest coverage, measuring how often the company could pay its annual interest expenses with the same year's EBIT. The model will base its estimation of debt capacity solely on this ratio and the rating that the investors would like to target for the company. This has two shortcomings. First, it ignores all other factors linked to ratings as listed above; second, it works less well for young or growing firms whose historic EBIT results might be volatile or have bad predictions for the future. Regarding the first shortcoming we can note that the EBIT coverage ratio is in most cases the dominant credit quality criteria and is also used as sole parameter in many applications of synthetic rating estimation.[124] Regarding the second shortcoming relating to younger and fast growing firms, we have to think about adjustments, specifically as it relates to technology companies. Damodaran makes the following suggestion in that context: "In these cases, an estimated synthetic rating can be based on the expected interest coverage ratio over the next few years, rather than the current interest coverage ratio."[125] However, basing debt capacity on projected fast growth a few years out might in many cases not convince rating agencies or lenders who are more interested in current or near term cash flows. A

---

[124] Damodaran, The dark side of valuation, p. 89.
[125] Damodaran, The dark side of valuation, pp. 89-90.

compromise that has been incorporated into the model uses the first year predicted EBIT to determine the leverage. Assuming that the first model year is the first year of the buyout, the coverage ratio will never be lower than the stated minimum to maintain the company's rating.[126]

We can conclude that by reversing synthetic rating estimation, the model approximates the debt capacity. It does so through a bottom-up approach using the predicted EBIT in the first year of the buyout. This way, the amount of debt to finance the buyout can be derived. Having found a way to raise debt, in the next step we focus on the opposite: How to repay the debt?

5.3 Projections

Pro-forma projections in finance are forecasts of financial statements and reports following a certain methodology. Much of this methodology is already incorporated in the definitions and workings of financial statements. For instance, capital expenditures above depreciation are defined as net capital expenditures. When calculating free cash flows from net income, it is therefore sufficient to only subtract net capital expenditures, since the to be added depreciation cancels out all capital expenditures up to the effective net capital expenditures.

The following table shows the pro-forma statements of the model projected over the assumed horizon of the buyout, using data from German database and XML solutions provider Software AG for demonstration:

[126] Model sheet ValuationLBO shows the interest coverage ratio for each year over the buyout horizon.

	0	1	2	3	4	5
	2001a	2002e	2003e	2004e	2005e	2006e
Income Statement						
Sales	416.6	479.1	551.0	633.6	728.7	838.0
EBIT	113.8	130.8	150.4	173.0	199.0	228.8
- Interest expenses		37.4	23.8	18.9	12.8	5.5
= Pretax Income		93.4	126.6	154.2	186.1	223.3
- Income taxes		31.8	43.1	52.4	63.3	75.9
= Net Income		61.7	83.6	101.7	122.9	147.4
Cash Flow Statement						
Net Income		61.7	83.6	101.7	122.9	147.4
+ Amortization of Transaction Costs		5.9	5.9	5.9	5.9	5.9
+ Proceeds from Asset Sale & Excess Cash		137.9	0.0	0.0	0.0	0.0
- Increase in Net Working Capital		0.3	0.4	0.4	0.5	0.5
- Net Capital Expenditures (after Depreciation)		15.6	18.0	20.7	23.8	27.3
- Increase in Cash Reserve		2.5	2.9	3.3	3.8	4.4
= CFBDR (Cash Flow Before Debt Repayment)		187.1	68.3	83.3	100.8	121.1
- Debt Repayment		187.1	68.3	83.3	100.8	76.1
= Balance available for additional CapEx		0.0	0.0	0.0	0.0	44.9
Cash Account						
Beginning Cash		16.7	19.2	22.0	25.3	29.1
+ Increase in Cash Reserve		2.5	2.9	3.3	3.8	4.4
= Ending Cash		19.2	22.0	25.3	29.1	33.5
Capitalization						
Total Debt	515.6	328.5	260.2	176.9	76.1	0.0
Equity	507.0	568.7	652.2	754.0	876.8	1,024.2
Total Capitalization	1,022.5	897.1	912.4	930.8	952.9	1,024.2
D/(D+E)	0.50	0.37	0.29	0.19	0.08	0.00

Figure 9: Projections (data from Software AG)

It is apparent that other than general accounting and finance principles, a set of 'rules' must define how the projections develop. In summary, these are:

- Constant sales growth
- Constant EBIT margin
- Buyout takes place at the end of base year

Let us consider the first part of the projections, the income statement. The income statement begins with the most recent sales and EBIT figures as entered in the InputsLBO sheet of the model. The assumption is that the buyout takes place at the beginning of the year following the base year for which the financials are known. Ideally, the model is being used on the 31st of December, incorporates the financials of the ending year, and emulates a buyout that begins on the following day, the first of January of the new year. In reality, the reporting of financials, the application of the model, and the planned buyout are usually apart in time, thus making this not too much of a realistic scenario. It appears intuitive, however, that the benefits of attempting to incorporate the exact timing of financial reports, model application, and buyout would be minimal compared to the added layer of complexity. Additionally, the fact that a significant number of companies have financial years not in line with calendar years, would add further difficulties to that attempt.

Once we know the base year sales and EBIT, we can project the sales over the buyout horizon given the constant growth rate. Since the EBIT margin remains constant at the level of the base year, EBIT growth is at the same rate as sales growth. To avoid circularity, interest expenses, being the first item to be subtracted from EBIT, are calculated on the basis of the outstanding debt of the previous year.[127]

The cash flow statement carries one item that has not yet been discussed and seems unusual in this place: proceeds from asset sale & excess cash. The first part relates to after-tax proceeds of asset sales that often follow buyouts. As there is no apparent and systematic way of estimating the asset sale potential in a standardized model, this field (and the accompanying input field) only exists for individual analysis of a company and has zero value otherwise. The proceeds from excess cash, however, are incorporated into the standardized model since they can easily be derived, and because excess cash is an important value

[127] This follows a suggestion from Baldwin. See: Baldwin, Technical note on LBO valuation (A), p. 3.

component for companies with negative enterprise values.[128] Items to be subtracted from the net income include increase in net working capital, net capital expenditures and increase in cash reserve (all by the ratios as assumed in the InputsLBO sheet). Afterward, the cash flow available for debt repayment will be used to pay down debt and the balance should be zero.[129]

It should be noted that the equity in the capitalization calculation is the book equity, which is increasing with net income. The effective equity available to shareholders will only be known at the exit event of the company subsequent to the buyout horizon. The beauty of pro-forma models is that once working rules and a set of inputs and assumptions has been established, the models run by themselves.

We finally arrive at four figures in the last year of the buyout horizon that are crucial to determining the price at which the company can be sold: Sales, EBIT, cash on hand, and remaining debt. Equipped with these numbers, we can confidently approach the next step of the buyout model.

5.4 Valuation

Since the model was built on the Equity Cash Flow method and IRR discount rate, we can estimate the return to investors using the equity cash flow events of a buyout, acquisition and divestment (exit). The figure below shows the cash flows to the equity investors excluding management (net cash flows to the LBO fund):

---

[128] We will discuss their valuation within the model in section 5.5.

[129] The special case of a positive balance will also be examined in section 5.5.

Valuation

Equity Value	**791.7**
+ Acquisition Premium	197.9
+ Transaction Costs	29.7
= Total Equity Acquisition Price	1,019.3
- New Debt	512.3
= Initial Acquirer Equity	507.0
- Management Participation	24.3
= Initial Investor Equity	**482.6**

Enterprise Value of Exit	**1,915.1**
- Debt	0.0
+ Cash	33.5
= Proceeds to Equity Holders	1,948.6
- Proceeds to Management	155.9
= Proceeds to Investor	**1,792.7**

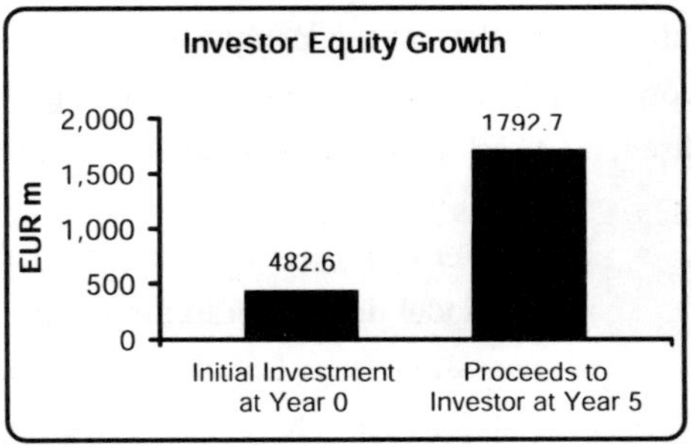

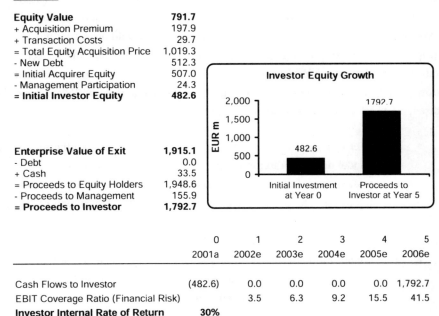

	0	1	2	3	4	5
	2001a	2002e	2003e	2004e	2005e	2006e
Cash Flows to Investor	(482.6)	0.0	0.0	0.0	0.0	1,792.7
EBIT Coverage Ratio (Financial Risk)		3.5	6.3	9.2	15.5	41.5
Investor Internal Rate of Return	**30%**					

Figure 10: Valuation (data from Software AG)

The calculations to arrive at the first LBO investor cash flow simply add the acquisition price to be paid for 100% control of the equity, and subtract the debt that can be raised to help finance the deal as well as the management equity contribution. If a company has a high debt capacity and little existing debt, the power of leverage can easily be seen in the drastically reduced acquisition price for the equity investors.

Due to the cash sweep covenants typically used for LBOs, all cash flows will be used to repay debt and none goes back to equity holders during the buyout. Therefore, the cash flows of the first to fourth year are zero. For the fifth year, the model assumes the exit event for equity holders, either through a trade sale, an initial public offering, a secondary buyout, a leveraged recapitalization or other forms of ownership change. The questions are how we can value the equity, and for how much the company could ultimately be sold for in five years time. As discussed in the overview of leveraged buyout valuation, several methods exist to determine the value in five years time. One way would be to continue the cash flow model, find a target debt-to-capital ratio and discount the expected future cash flows at the Weighted Average Costs of Capital, or use another cash flow based approach. However, valuing the company at the exit via a new discounted cash flow analysis has shortcomings:

- It is easier to project the company's cash flows five years into the future, as the model does, than to project the cash flows into infinity, as it would be necessary in a full discounted cash flow valuation. Often, difficult assumptions have to be made about the length of the high-growth period and the terminal value thereafter.

- Since we are estimating for how much the company could sell at the end of the buyout, we need to focus on how new buyers might value the company. In practice, discounted cash flow analysis is more often conducted to rationalize a price that has already been derived in other ways, mostly through multiples analysis. Especially for initial public offerings, but also for mergers & acquisitions, discounted cash flow analysis has more a supporting role; there are both empirical and theoretical indications that the value is mainly derived via multiples.[130]

[130] Many academics would oppose this practice: "Multiples should never be your only valuation method and preferably not even your primary focus." Benninga/Sarig: corporate finance – a valuation approach, p. 305. On the other hand, Damodaran points out, that "[...] a relative [multiple based] valuation is much more likely to reflect the current mood of the market, since it is an attempt to measure relative and not intrinsic value". Damodaran, The dark side of valuation, p. 252. Indications for a dominant role of multiples in valuation can also be found in the high-flying valuations of newly listed technology companies in 1999 and 2000. Analysts and IPO bankers were adjusting their discounted cash flow models with questionable growth assumptions (and sometimes even real options as discussed later) to bring them in line with the value derived from multiples of comparable companies.

At the end of the day, the market value of a firm is what buyers are willing to pay.[131]

It can be argued, therefore, that a better approach for deriving a fair exit value is the use of relative valuation. One more factor that speaks for using multiples, particularly in our model, is the following: Since LBO investors and management have acquired the company at certain multiples, we already know a set of multiples that we can use to value the exit. We do not even have to look for other comparable firms, as we already have transaction multiples of exactly the firm that we need to value. Further, this approach is very conservative: Usually companies going through an LBO are acquired at low multiples compared to their peer-group. Undervaluation was in fact one of the value drivers for LBOs that was previously identified. Since the LBO investors thought to make a good deal at the acquisition multiples they paid for the company, it is reasonable to assume that the company would be bought at least at these multiples. In fact, LBO investors hope to sell at better multiples, and most often they can, if their plan to improve efficiency in operations, to incentive management and to pursue a long-term strategy for the company can be executed. However, to calculate conservatively and not assume an overly optimistic exit price, the model assumes the same exit multiples as acquisition multiples. This is in line with practitioners who advise not to "assume an exit multiple that is higher than your buy-in multiple".[132]

What multiples should we use for the model? The three major multiples that could be utilized would be:

- Enterprise Value / Sales
- Enterprise Value / EBIT
- Market Capitalization / Net Income or Price per share / Earnings per share

---

[131] Some efficient market proponents would argue that the current market value of a company equals the discounted cash flow value at any time, and therefore relative valuation and discounted cash flow valuation would always yield the same company value.

[132] Richerstein, Buyout, p. 188.

The EV (EV for enterprise value) / Sales multiples has the advantage that it ignores differences in accounting practices in individual firms and can be applied independently of whether a company is profitable. It has been the dominant multiple to value unprofitable technology companies for this reason. However, its advantages are also part of its weaknesses, since EV/Sales ignores a company's operating efficiency and its margins, as well as its earnings growth prospects and capital investments.[133]

Both the EV/Sales and EV/EBIT multiple are independent of the capital structure of a firm, since they are derived from the enterprise value. This is conceptually sound, because the EBIT or sales generated by a company's assets belong to both debt and equity holders. In opposition to EV/Sales, EV/EBIT has the advantage of providing meaningful information about a company's profitability.

One more step down the balance sheet would be the market capitalization / net income ratio, commonly expressed with per share values as price/earnings (PE). Since the net income is the residual income after debt holders have been paid, it is measured against the firm's equity expressed as market capitalization or share price and not the enterprise value. The PE, being the "most widely used and misused of all multiples"[134], has some shortcomings though, especially when used for technology companies. As with any ratio, the PE requires positive numbers as inputs and therefore it cannot take companies into account that have negative net income, which is more often the case in the technology sector than in traditional industry sectors. Net income is also strongly influenced by accounting techniques and so-called extraordinary items such as restructuring costs or acquisition costs, making the PE sometimes a weak indicator of a firm's true operating profitability.[135]

---

[133] See Benninga, Coroporate finance: A valuation approach, p. 326.

[134] Damodaran, the dark side of valuation, p. 275.

[135] Whether extraordinary items are that extraordinary indeed is another discussion. Financial analysts frequently try to exclude those items in their analysis, leading companies to increasingly declare as many expenses as possible to be extraordinary. See Peoplesoft's recent troubles in claiming their product development expenses to be extraordinary, MacDonald, PeopleShell?, pp. 93, 94. Another point supporting the shortcoming of net

Although each of the discussed multiples would work for the model and has its own advantages and disadvantages, the exit value at the end of the buyout horizon will be calculated using EV/EBIT. It is less influenced by accounting practices and short-term factors and at the same time carries more meaning than a sales multiple. Therefore, the final calculation for the cash flow to equity holders is:

EBIT of year 5 *EBIT multiple at acquisition = exit enterprise value

Subtracting the net debt (debt minus cash) will then give the assumed exit cash flow to equity holders.[136] Thereafter, we can easily calculate the IRR with the formula already introduced in section 4.4. Overall, the model allows for an estimation of the IRR of the buyout with little company information supplied. Further, based on general assumptions about the structure of an LBO, we are able to establish how profitable an investment might be.

5.5 Special Cases

The model has been adjusted to provide workable results in three special cases, each of which might otherwise lead to incorrect or meaningless outcomes:

- Enterprise value is negative
- EBIT is too low to fund assumed sales growth
- Additional debt capacity is higher than acquisition price

The enterprise value of a company is negative when the following equation is less than zero:

---

income as an unbiased value indication is the practice to manage net income in various situations. In management changes, the new CEO often aims for a low net income in his/her first year, clearing all hidden earning problems of the past and giving him or herself upward space to increase earnings. Earnings are also significantly influenced by merges & acquisitions, as well as restructuring charges that make them a problematic indicator of firm profitability.

136 Note that this calculation of enterprise value ignores minority interest, in opposition to the enterprise value calculated at the time of acquisition, since there will be no minority interest following the acquisition.

enterprise value = market capitalization + debt + minority interest – cash

Ignoring minority interest, a negative enterprise value exists when there is more cash than there is market capitalization and outstanding debt. Following the downturn in technology stocks beginning in March 2000, a number of companies that had often raised money just shortly before faced dramatically falling valuations, this while still having substantial IPO proceeds in their cash account. This phenomenon led to publicly listed firms – in 2001 their number was about 200[137] – that were trading below the value of the cash (called 'lucky buys'), and analysts and press have since discussed its implications.[138] "When a company sells for less than its cash, investors are essentially saying the company's business is worth less than zero. Theoretically, an investor could buy up all the stock, shut down the company and walk away with a profit, though in reality, the costs of closing up shop would likely wipe away any gains."[139]

However, it is not only potentially high closure costs that could help explain why acquirers have not yet seized these seeming opportunities. On the one hand, due to the high cash accounts sellers often see no need to sell, especially at these valuations. On the other hand, buyers are hesitant to buy when they expect the price to fall further – 'why buy now if we can get it cheaper later?' Another explanation for negative enterprise values of some companies are substantial off-balance sheet liabilities that are not included in the calculation for the enterprise value but would have to be assumed by an acquirer. Additionally, the overall poor economic visibility, the inability of some of those companies to even generate meaningful revenues, and potential conflicts with management (often

137 See: Brown, Some cheap firms still don't seem to find any takers, p. 16. In section 7.2 an analysis of technology companies with negative enterprise values is provided, estimating the aggregated negative value of the top 30 negative enterprise value companies at over EUR 1 billion.

138 One of the most detailed research efforts in that context was conducted by analysts of Dresdner Kleinwort Wasserstein who estimated cash burn rates and 'lucky buy' potential for German Neuer Markt listed companies. See: Dresdner Kleinwort Wasserstein (Ed.), German Neuer Markt: The price of growth.

139 Brown, Some cheap firms still don't seem to find any takers, p. 16.

the largest shareholder) are further factors that might help explain a phenomenon not possible in financial text book markets.

How can the model accommodate negative enterprise values? There are two issues the model needs to address. It must find a way to deal with the cash and to value the company at the exit (since we have no EV/EBIT acquisition multiple due to the negative EV at the time of acquisition). For the latter, we will have to assume a fixed EV/EBIT exit multiple and enter it into the InputsLBO sheet. Dealing with the cash account that is worth more than equity and debt together is slightly more complicated. Theoretically, investors could make an instant arbitrage profit. For the reasons cited above, however, this is not realistic in most cases. The cash account, therefore, will not be given to the equity investors at the time of acquisition or be used to finance the acquisition, but will be reinvested instead in the company, first as debt repayment and then as capital expenditures for the remaining funds. All cash above the required cash on hand and after debt repayment, defined as excess cash, will be added to the net capital expenditures in the first year of the buyout, thus leading to sales growth at the "sales growth from excess cash rate" as assumed in the InputsLBO sheet. This way the model can include companies in the analysis that have a negative enterprise value at the time of the acquisition. Note that this approach is actually conservative, as we view the excess cash to be part of the company's operations and therefore not to be directly available to shareholders.

Another special case exists if a company's EBIT margin of the base year (and therefore the margin of all other years) is too low to fund sales growth at the assumed constant sales growth rate, i.e. if the required increase in net working capital, cash on hand and net capital expenditures cannot be paid by the available net income.[140] To avoid negative cash flows and not to add intra buyout financing, the added sum of these items will never be higher than the available net income. Some items, then, could be lower than what they should be according to the assumptions. We could interpret this case as increased efficiency

140 As described in section 5.3, these are all variables of sales growth.

or costs saving measurements. Additionally, this situation would most often exist when excess cash has caused strong sales growth, and is therefore compensated by the very conservative assumption about excess cash reinvestment.[141]

A situation that should theoretically not exist, similar to a negative enterprise value, is when a firm could be completely financed by the debt it could raise on its cash flows and assets; put another way, when the debt capacity, minus its pre-existing debt, is greater than its acquisition price. In order to have a negative cash flow for equity investors at the time of the acquisition, the InputsLBO sheet provides a field called "minimum equity in % of acquisition price". The default setting should be at least 10%. Thus in case a company could technically be bought purely by the debt raised for it, equity investors would have to pay at least 10% of the acquisition price.[142]

Obviously, companies that have negative EBIT are excluded from the model and the IRR will be zero for them, since they would in most cases not be able to assume substantial amounts of debt. Although this will be the case for a significant number of technology companies, it reflects the goal of the model to analyze attractiveness for a leveraged buyout of technology companies, even if few fill that criterion. It should be noted that in some cases – and speaking purely technically – companies might provide attractive buyout opportunities, even though they have negative operating income. This is the case, for example, when a company's negative enterprise value provides sufficient return by itself, even if the company is not profitable.

---

141 Making the sales growth dependent on the available funding for these items in the same year would cause circularity. Obviously, there would be ways around this, such as iteration, shifting in timing of either sales growth or sales growth funding items etc.; however, the benefits can be regarded as rather small relative to the complication they would cause in the model.

142 Note that this scenario is independent of any rating issue and does not mean a company would be overly in debt. Rather it could result from a severe undervaluation that should, however, occur rarely in practice. Since undervalued companies are the focus of the model, this eventuality has been incorporated.

Naturally, the model works with both private and public companies. Instead of the current market capitalization plus the premium, the trading price will need to be input for a private acquisition such as a spin-off or corporate disposal, leading to results no different than in the case of a public company.

5.6 Model Limitations

Given the assumptions and workings of the developed model, it is apparent that its application is subject to some rigid limitations. As in most models, the limitations are largely a product of constraints that were established, so that the model could serve a specific goal. In our case, it is the goal to make the model applicable to any company in various situations using only six variable inputs that can be easily obtained. The major limitations of the model can be summarized as follows:

- The model assumes that sales and EBIT will grow at a constant rate. In reality, this will never be the case. The question is whether this can sufficiently serve as a proxy for the real future cash flows. In some cases, it will certainly not.

- The attractiveness evaluation is not risk-adjusted. Assuming comparable operational risks of the analyzed companies and the same financial risk due to a chosen credit rating, the IRR can approximate attractiveness, though final determination depends on the specific hurdle rate set.

- All inputs are a one-time picture at a given moment. They might therefore represent a rare or atypical situation. For example, if a company had atypically high or low sales in the last available financial year, this non-average figure will be the basis for cash flow projections.

- The debt capacity only depends on the most recent operating profit. Given the currently low interest rates, some companies might be able to assume more debt by their interest coverage ratio than they were by other ratios such as existing leverage. Other companies with unusually low EBIT might be underleveraged in the model.

- All inputs are accounting data (except market capitalization). Accounting data is subject to a certain degree of interpretation as well as different accounting standards.[143]

- Although companies with negative enterprise values can be included, their evaluation would depend essentially on the growth rate they can generate with their excess cash. This assumption leads us to ask why the companies have not already invested that cash to achieve that growth. In other cases, the model might undervalue existing cash positions.

- Finally, the model does not take into account relative valuation. Since the exit multiple is the same as the entrance multiple, the valuation of a company compared to its peers does not influence the IRR. Obviously, though, a relatively 'cheap' company is more attractive than an 'expensive' one, since the downside is more secure while the exit upside has more potential.[144]

The chosen high degree of abstraction inevitably leads to a loss of precision and exactness in the individual case. The model's results must be evaluated with these limitations in mind.

---

[143] However, most technology companies in Europe, follow IAS or US-GAAP by now, often a stipulation of the so called European New Markets.

[144] In section 7.1, "Model Extension", we will attempt to account for this limitation.

6 Adjusting for Technology Risk and Return

Thus far we have developed a simplified buyout model that can be applied to various buyout situations in various industries. Although some of the assumptions of the model were already made with respect to technology buyouts, we have not yet asked how the model as a whole could be adjusted for technology firms, or rather what the key issues are when applying this model to technology firms. As seen, technology firms are subject to specific risks, which is the reason they have traditionally been avoided by buyout investors. They also represent particular return opportunities due to the growth upside, which have historically outpaced by far most firms in traditional industries. In the following section, we evaluate how an application of the model would need to be adjusted to the technology-specific risk and return characteristics.

Having provided little information about technology buyouts in general, it is no wonder literature provides even less on the valuation of technology buyouts. One of the few references comes from Robbie/Wright/Albrighton and is based on an empirical analysis of 337 "high-tech" buyouts in the UK from 1991 until 1996. The findings are surprising: "[...] for the high-tech group, liquidation emerged as the most important (26%) [method of valuation] followed by book value (24%), discounted cash flow techniques (21%), recent transaction prices of companies in the same sector (13%) and capitalized earnings (11%)."[145] These results, the paper continues, support the authors' view that "the valuation of high-tech buy-outs is significantly more likely to make use of liquidation values than is the case for non-high-tech buyouts."[146]

The empirical study of Robbie/Wright/Albrighton leaves some questions. First, a limitation that might have made the results non-representative was the fact that of the 337 companies contacted for the study, only 40 provided information that entered into the results. Furthermore, no information was given on the average firm size or the rationale behind the buyout; therefore some of the buyouts could

145 Robbie/Wright/Albrighton, High-tech management buy-outs, p. 229.
146 Robbie/Wright/Albrighton, High-tech management buy-outs, p. 222.

represent a turnaround situation for which a liquidation value is indeed more often used.[147] Other factors outside the study justify further skepticism towards the above findings. Liquidation and book values of technology companies are, as mentioned, usually the smallest source of their market value. Today the majority of technology companies still trades at price-to-book multiples substantially above market averages, indicating the prevailing perception that the value of a technology company's current and future cash flows is generated predominantly by intangible assets. It is therefore hard to understand why the sellers of the sampled buyouts would have sold at liquidation value, that being the lowest possible value a seller would always receive. In the end, sample size, missing information on the true nature of the buyouts and a valuation opposing historic and current market conditions in the technology markets make the findings of this empirical study not of meaningful help in understanding technology buyout valuation. It is unfortunate that this is, for the time being, the only systematic study of its kind.

Rather than looking at empirical indications, we will approach the adjustment issue based on valuation theory and practical applicability. As we will see, the "difference" of technology buyouts can, to some extent, be incorporated into a valuation model.

6.1 Technology Risk

In section 3.1 we elaborated on the sources of risk that are unique to technology buyouts, as opposed to buyouts in traditional and mature industries. There are

[147] Robbie/Wright/Albrighton do investigate the motivation behind the buyout of their sample group, but these findings do not provide real insight in that respect. The only agreement among the firms, when questioned about the management motivation for the buyout, was that the majority disagreed with the answers provided by Robbie/Wright/Albrighton. See: Robbie/Wright/Albrighton, High-tech management buy-outs, p. 230. Other than the fact that non-core business divesture played a major role for the vendor motivation, it is hard to conclude the real nature of the sampled buyouts. In the end, only one source of motivation remains with some degree of significance: "Managers effecting high-tech buy-outs are significantly more likely than managers effecting non-high-tech buy-outs to be motivated by the desire to exploit technology-related opportunities." Robbie/Wright/Albrighton, High-tech management buy-outs, p. 221. This should be hardly surprising, given the fact that technology buyouts are the object of the study.

many ways in corporate finance valuation to account for higher perceived risk of an asset or higher "degree of uncertainty of return on an asset".[148] The key in risk adjustment is transparency, which allows a rational appraisal of the perceived risk. Once the cloud of risk has been made transparent, the risk factors can be addressed and incorporated into the valuation. The following section briefly describes the parameters that can be adjusted in a buyout model to reflect technology risk.

6.1.1 Increase Hurdle Rate

We have said that the projected IRR of an investment is compared to a hurdle or required IRR, reflecting an investment's risks and the return requirements of the LBO fund. An obvious way to account for higher perceived risk is to increase the hurdle rate for an investment. A reasonable approach could be to increase the required rate of return for technology buyouts over that of traditional buyouts with similar leverage to the level, at which the risk-return perception of the investor, once the technology-specific risk has been adjusted, is equal. In other words, we ask: How much more must the investment earn, to have an equally attractive risk-return payoff as an otherwise comparable non-technology investment? The difference in required returns could then be called a technology buyout risk premium.

There are two obstacles to such a concept, however. On the one hand, there is barely any empirical data available for estimating such a premium based on past transactions. On the other hand, the required return also depends largely on the perceived risk of the individual investment – even across an investment class such as technology buyouts, the individual risk patterns differ substantially.[149] It should also be noted that academics voice strong criticism to "arbitrarily" made adjustments to discount rates that are not derived in the first place from an asset

148 Harvey, Hypertextual finance glossary, w/o pg.

149 Another difficulty would be the overall problem in private equity that investors do not disclose their target returns when making investments.

pricing model.[150] Rather, they argue, in order to account for higher levels of risk, the projections for future cash flows should be adjusted.[151]

6.1.2 Lower Cash Flow Projections

The cash flows of a well-constructed discounted cash flow model should reflect the expected cash flows of all possible outcomes. If, for instance, the possibility of an outperforming cash flow arises for a certain year, this cash flow weighted by its likelihood should enter the expected cash flow for that year.[152] In fact, the strongest argument against exogenous additions to the discounted cash flow (DCF) model can be made by pointing to the fact that everything with impact on value should be priced into DCF analysis.[153] Scenario analysis and sensitivity analysis using Monte Carlo simulation, for instance, are two approaches that can incorporate wider ranges of cash flow relevant information into the projections and increase the likelihood that the expected cash flows will be close to real cash flows.[154] Valuing technology buyouts should not make a difference in that respect. The technology related risks have to be rationalized and their impact on the expected future cash flow estimated. Substantial cash flow discounts could be the result of such analysis in order to reflect higher risk. Worst case scenarios could be given more weight to arrive at lower expected cash flow projections.

---

150 This can also be seen as a general criticism on the IRR approach. However, in section 4.4 we mentioned that the IRR can be understood as indirectly derived from the CAPM.

151 "Managers often add fudge factors to discount rates to offset worries [of risk] [...]. This sort of adjustment makes us nervous", say Brealey/Myers and outline further: "Don't give in to the temptation to add fudge factors to the discount rate to offset things that could go wrong with the proposed investment." Brealey/Myers, The principles of corporate finance, p. 238.

152 See: Nygard/Razaire, Probability-based DCF: An alternative to point-value estimates, p. 69. A practical application of probability weighted cash flow analysis for technology projects and specifically R&D is provided in: Boer, The valuation of technology, p. 293.

153 This should theoretically also include options and other up or down side scenarios. Opponents would argue that some of these values, especially options, cannot always be incorporated into DCF and must be treated separately. See: Copeland/Koller/Murrin, Valuation: measuring and managing the value of companies, p. 470; Brealey/Meyer: Principles of corporate finance, p. 620.

154 Scenario analysis projects probability weighted scenarios whereas Monte Carlo simulation considers all possible combinations of input variables. Both can easily been conducted today with advanced software products such as Crystal Ball, http://www.decisioneering.com. See: Li, Simple computer applications improve the versatility of discounted cash flow analysis, pp. 86-92.

Quantifying the discount, however, is a difficult and ultimately subjective process. A short cut could be a post valuation adjustment for the likelihood of failure, where we increase the probability of failure above the level of traditional buyouts:

Adjusted technology buyout value =
DCF Value * (1-probability of failure) + liquidation value * probability of failure[155]

Using this formula, technology risk could not only be reflected by a higher assumed failure probability, but also by the generally significantly lower liquidation value of technology companies. Estimating failure probabilities, however, would not always be easier than adjusting the cash flows themselves. Overall, it seems that although cash flow adjustments are the theoretically most correct way to accommodate for firm specific technology risk, their application remains challenging admit estimating a single cash flow projection that incorporates various sources of uncertainty.

6.1.3 Increase Cost of Debt

Technology firms are on average less levered than the rest of the economy.[156] This results partly from the lack of tangible assets that could serve as covenants to lenders, but more so from higher revenue and earning volatility that might put the debt serving ability of technology firms at risk.[157] Although no empirical data is available on the average debt terms of the past technology buyouts, cost of

---

[155] This formula follows Damodaran's proposal to adjust for the likelihood of failure. In his analysis of technology companies, however, he does not apply this approach, because he believes he already incorporated the chance of failure into the cash flow projections. Damodaran, The dark side of valuation, p. 209. The risk of failure that might be higher for technology companies should only be estimated with this formula, if it has been excluded from the cash flow projections before.

[156] A screening of 700 European technology and communication firms in major growth indices provided an average after cash leverage of 14.96 % of total market capitalization (data compiled from Bloomberg, outliers excluded, 01.02.2002).

[157] Another reason for the low leverage among technology companies can also be seen in the historically abundant availability of equity capital for technology companies. The high volatility argument has been opposed by Deb/Kesavan as briefly discussed in section 3.1.

debt is generally higher for technology firms, while debt capacity is lower.[158] In the end, "LBO funds cannot secure as much leverage for a technology company as they can for a more traditional target."[159] Therefore, when we model a technology buyout, the interest coverage ratio should be higher compared to the average in its corporate rating class, and the debt spread should be at the upper end of its rating class. Finally, the rating itself must reflect the credit market conditions for technology firms. By choosing an investment grade rating for the model above the usual LBO below investment grade target rating, we adjust for the technology-specific risk that lenders perceive in such transactions.

6.1.4 Plan for Investments

Growth does not come free; it ultimately is determined by how much is (re)invested and the quality of these investments.[160] The higher average growth rates of technology companies are financed by higher capital investments and R&D expenses. Therefore, when projecting growth rates reflecting higher average growth of technology companies, the reinvestment rate of technology buyouts must be above the rate of traditional buyouts. In the model, we approximate the capital requirements for sales growth by using a net capital expenditure / sales growth ratio that should at least be the average of the specific technology segment.[161] The ratio can even be significantly higher, if an increase in capital spending and R&D is part of the buyout plan, as it was for instance in the Seagate buyout: "By going private, Seagate might be able to aggressively pursue investments that had longer-term payoffs."[162] Using high capital spending

---

[158] "LBO firms have traditionally avoided companies with even a small technological component because the debt markets considered their cash flows less reliable than those of more mainstream businesses [...]." Gove, Raiding the valley, w/o pg. Texas Pacific Group had for its three first technology transactions debt ratios of 2:1, 1:1 and 0, indicating the on average limited debt accessibility for technology buyouts compared to traditional buyouts. Gove, Raiding the valley, w/o pg.

[159] Gove, Raiding the valley, w/o pg.

[160] See: Damodaran, The dark side of valuation, p. 142.

[161] Since the model did not differentiate the market segments in the technology sector, an overall average was assumed.

[162] Once Seagate was taken private, "it would 'invest like crazy' in new product development and manufacturing facilities." Both quotes from: Andrade/Gilson/Pulvino, Seagate Technology Buyout, p. 7.

assumptions helps also to account for product replacement risk and short product life cycles. Variables such as capital expenditures that can be adjusted to the demands of technology companies provide a transparent way of addressing certain risk factors and incorporating them into cash flow projections. Adjusting cash flows this way is more rational than a brute force discount or a failure probability, but whether it can sufficiently reflect all technology-specific risk is questionable.

6.2 Technology Return

As much as there is a need to price the risks specific to technology companies into buyout valuation, it also is necessary to incorporate the return potential. This is why investors pursue these opportunities, even though the risk level is higher than that of traditional buyouts.

What drives the upside of a technology buyout? In the end, it comes down to one factor: growth. The following briefly describes two ways of incorporating the return potential specific to technology buyouts into a valuation model.

6.2.1 Increase Growth Rate

Since the technology industry has historically grown at much higher rates than the rest of the economy, much of the rationale for technology buyout investing is based on the ability of technology companies to grow faster than companies in traditional industries. The growth potential may in fact outpace the discussed risk factors and make an investment worth pursuing. It is essential to determine a sound growth figure whose assumptions can be rationalized. As previously mentioned, growth is driven by investment and the quality of the investment. We can easily project how much a target company should invest to grow, but the difficulty lies in estimating how these investments pay off and translate into growth. A rational approach could be based on two steps. The first step involves estimating the growth of the market in which the company operates. Although we can say that technology on average grows significantly faster than the rest of the economy, growth rates vary substantially across the technology sector; therefore a segment specific growth rate provides a better proxy. The second step requires us to estimate whether the target is potentially able to grow faster or slower than its market. There might be good reasons for investors to believe a company could outperform its market, but the underlying factors for this must be separated and their impact individually analyzed. Finally, investors might hope that the company is able to enter or develop new markets and increase its growth beyond expectations based on technological innovation. Estimating this potential per se is challenging and its inclusion overly optimistic in most cases. Nevertheless, it makes sense to develop 'as if' scenarios and sensitivity analysis, so that the impact of excess growth on the IRR can be made transparent. Even though investors should not count on innovation based excess growth, the sheer potential for this is unique to technology buyouts and poses a significant part of their attractiveness.

6.2.2 Add Real Options

Another way of incorporating the return potential of technology buyouts might be achieved by the use of real options.[163] Real options are an extension of the financial derivatives theory to options on non-financial assets that are not included in DCF valuation according to proponents of real option theory.[164] There are two types of real options relevant to technology firms: the option to delay an investment into a technology or project and the option to expand into a new product or market resulting from an initial investment.[165] The option to delay would find use if a firm has exclusive rights to a project that might not be

[163] An option is a financial instrument whose value depends on the values of other, more basic underlying variables. E.g. a call option gives the holder the right, but not the obligation, to buy an underlying asset by a certain date for a certain price. See: Hull, Options, futures, & other derivatives, p. 6. Expanding on this understanding, real option is "the right, but not the obligation, to take action (e.g., deferring, expanding, contracting, or abandoning) at a predetermined cost called the exercise price, for a predetermined period of time – the life of the option." Copeland/Antikarov, Real options: a practitioner's guide, p. 5.

[164] In a more general context, Thomas notes: "By augmenting DCF analysis with real options analysis, executives can get a much clearer picture of the decision landscape they are facing. Best of all, the analysis produces quantitative, financial answers, linked to the financial market's valuation of return on investment and risk." Thomas, Business value analysis: coping with unruly uncertainty, p. 17.

[165] See: Damodaran, The dark side of valuation, p. 400.

attractive presently but could be later on.[166] More relevant in our case is the option to expand, especially for companies that operate in rapidly growing markets.

Real options became widely known in relation to their use for the valuation of Internet companies. As some analysts and academics found it difficult to justify stock prices of Internet companies with traditional DCF analysis during the late 1990s, some suggested assessing their value with real options. The argument was that traditional DCF analysis ignores the option value to expand into rapidly growing markets that is inherent in these firms.[167]

Similarly, when valuing technology buyouts, we could add real option value to the DCF value of a company to incorporate the possibility that a technology firm produces excess growth because it could innovate and expand into new markets. However, apart from the fact that the inputs required for real option valuation have a high degree of subjectivity[168] and that the option itself must be of proprietary nature as well as executable, an addition of real option value to the DCF value would only be justifiable if the firm has been clearly undervalued by DCF analysis in the first place. However, if we have incorporated all upside, which can be reasonably included in the cash flows of the DCF valuation, the application of real options would result in an overly optimistic valuation: i.e., we would double-count real option values. Therefore, we can conclude that even though real options might be a working approach in certain cases, their application is arbitrary and would be inconsistent when applied with a valuation

166 Patents on technology, especially in biotechnology can be valued this way.

167 A popular paper on valuing Internet companies with real options concluded that "depending on the parameters chosen and given high enough growth rates of revenues, the value of an Internet stock may be rational." Schwartz/Moon, Rational pricing of Internet companies, p. 74.

168 Real options, most commonly priced using the Black-Scholes pricing formula, also require all the inputs of that model. For the inputs see: Black/Scholes, The valuation of option contracts and a test of market efficiency, pp. 399-417.

approach that already incorporates upside potential to the extent that it should be done.[169]

6.3 Implications

We have seen that there are ways to accommodate the special risk and return nature of technology buyouts. Resulting from these findings, the developed LBO model was adjusted in the following ways:

- Since the IRR is the output of the model and the model itself does not suggest whether the achievable IRR indicates a good or bad opportunity, the model cannot and should not make any adjustments in that respect. It is the investor who sets the required IRR against which the output of the model is benchmarked. Our findings were that investors might raise their hurdle rate for a technology buyout above the level of a traditional buyout.

- The model does not include any technology discount on the projected cash flows or an adjusted value based on a failure probability. Although both would be possible and in some cases justified, applying them in a standardized way for all applications overly underestimates the average cash flows. Moreover, we assumed that the model's projections fairly reflect the expected future development of a company.

- The model does incorporate some degree of product development and life cycle risk by assuming higher than average capital expenditures, as input in the InputsLBO sheet. The net capital expenditures to sales growth ratio allows for a provision of additional investment resources to cover technology-specific investment requirements.

[169] There are two applications of real options that are generally more accepted: First, they are increasingly used for the valuation of projects that are driven by the price of a traded underlying, e.g., oil fields or gas power stations. Second, they can be a powerful tool in rationalizing and understanding the assumptions behind investments with a negative net present value that are nevertheless pursued for 'strategic reasons'.

- Given that no technology risk discount on the cash flow projections has been applied, it is also not wise to assume any overly optimistic growth rate to reflect upside potential. In specific cases this assumption might be justified, but for a standardized application, a growth rate on the lower end of the expected average industry growth as chosen in the model assumptions provides a fair balance between risk averseness and return pursuance.

- The model does not incorporate real options. They are, as outlined, controversial and arbitrary in this context. More important, they would overestimate the upside when a reasonable growth rate has already been defined. Further, a standardized application with real options hardly seems possible.

Overall, the attempt to include technology-specific risk and return characteristics has shown the limited degree to which these factors can be incorporated into a standardized model. The real message is that LBO investors must carefully measure the sources behind risk and return for technology companies, and must adjust their valuation for every case accordingly. The key adjustment factors in this process have been demonstrated.

7 European Technology Market Screening

So far we have developed an LBO model that can be applied in a standard form to any company and which requires only a few inputs that are easily obtained. Moreover, we have optimized the model for the valuation of technology buyouts to the extent possible and have highlighted key issues that could not be incorporated but should be taken into account by the investor when the model's output, the IRR, is compared. In the following sections, we apply the model to selected European Technology Markets. The aim is to (a) validate the model's application, and (b) identify companies that could be regarded as buyout opportunities. Finally, we will arrive at a short list of companies deemed good prospects by this model, which might provide further evidence about the degree of opportunity for buyouts in the European technology sector.

7.1 Model Extension

The output of the developed LBO model is the IRR, which tells us how attractive a buyout might be for a particular company. We have already noted that, in order to be applicable in a standardized way and keep a certain degree of simplicity, a number of limitations have to be made. To compensate for those limitations, as well as to allow further flexibility in defining buyout attractiveness, we extend the model to include additional attractiveness indicators whose impact on the final output can be freely adjusted. The additional parameters are summarized under three groups along with the reasoning for their inclusion given, followed by a table listing each parameter with a short rationale for its use:

- **Debt:** Since the LBO model determines the leverage ability of a target company only by its most recent EBIT, additional debt ratios are included to provide a more complete debt capacity evaluation.

- **Valuation:** The LBO model does not, as mentioned, account for the relative valuation of a company. However, since a low relative valuation of a company is another important parameter for buyout attractiveness, several multiples are included as further indicators.

- **Performance:** Since the input data for the LBO model is of a static nature, additional growth and profitability indicators are built in to further enhance the meaning of the results.

Parameter	**Description and Rationale**
D/(E+D)	The debt to capitalization ratio provides information on the existing book leverage of the company. It tells how much of the overall book capital of the firm is from debt. Obviously, for a buyout, a low Debt/(Equity+Debt) ratio is desirable, as more debt can be taken on to finance the acquisition.
Net Debt/MC	The net debt to market capitalization ratio is similar to the debt to capitalization ratio, but instead of the balance sheet leverage it provides the actual market leverage adjusted for cash holdings. Note that whereas the D/(E+D) ratio compares the book debt to the whole (book) capitalization, the net debt to market capitalization ratio only compares the net debt to the market value of the equity, but not the enterprise capitalization. As with the D/(E+D) ratio, a lower Net Debt/MC ratio makes a target more attractive.
Price/book	The price to book value is a classic criterion in traditional buyout valuation as it compares the possible liquidity value of the company (assuming the book value is close to the liquidation value) with the current market value. In asset stripping valuations this is a useful indicator; for technology firms that have little tangible assets however, the price to book ratio is usually high and of less importance. A low price to book ratio indicates buyout attraction.
Debt/EBIT	This ratio compares the debt value with the most current EBIT and says how many years it would take to pay off all existing debt using the current EBIT. Again, the lower the value, the more a company could be leveraged and the more attractive it is for a buyout.
PE	Price to earnings ratio was already part of the discussion in section 5.4, "Valuation". The general rule for all multiples (PE, EV/EBIT, EV/Sales) is that the lower the multiple, the lower is the relative valuation and hence the more attractive the company it would be for a buyout.
EV/EBIT	Enterprise value to EBIT ratio; already discussed in section 5.4, "Valuation".
EV/Sales	Enterprise value to Sales; already discussed in section 5.4, "Valuation".
Current vs 52 week low	This ratio equals the current stock price divided by the 52 week low. It tells how much above the 52 week low the stock of the company is currently trading. E.g. a current vs. 52 week low ratio of 1.5 means that the stock price is currently trading 50% above its 52 week low. Therefore, the lower this value, the more attractive the company might be, as it trades close to its lowest one year historic value.

Parameter	Description and Rationale
EBIT Margin	The EBIT margin is calculated by dividing EBIT by sales. Naturally, the higher the EBIT margin, the more attractive is the target.
EBIT growth	This parameter refers to the one year EBIT growth. Higher EBIT growth demonstrates positive dynamics in operating profit and is therefore attractive.
PEG	The price earnings to growth ratio divides the current price earnings multiple by the projected growth rate in earnings. A value below 1 indicates undervaluation, or more generally, the lower the PEG, the more attractive is the company as a target.[170]

Table 6: Additional attractiveness parameters

In order to rank companies according to their attractiveness – depending on the definition of the model user – the ideal would be to have only one output that takes into account all the parameters listed above and the IRR. The extended model allows for the scaling and weighting of all parameters, so that a single output can be generated for each company according to the scales and weights set by the user. Since all parameters provide very different values – some are ratios, others are growth rates, we need to find a way of comparing these parameters. This can be achieved by defining a value range for each parameter, where the highest value and everything above it becomes 100% 'attractiveness' (assuming the highest value to be the best) and the lowest value and everything below it is set to 0% 'attractiveness'. For instance, we might want to credit all companies with an IRR of 50% or more with 100%, and companies with an IRR of 10% or less with 0%.[171] This way, all values in between the assumed worst and best values become scaled from 0% to 100%.[172]

---

170 Although theoretically not fully consistent, due to the lack of available earnings projections, historic EBIT growth is used in the extended model to approximate projected earning growth. Furthermore, the PEG was grouped under 'performance' in the Excel model, but could also be grouped under 'valuation'.

171 If a lower value of a parameter means higher attractiveness, it works exactly the opposite way. E.g., if a company has a EV/Sales ratio of 0.2 or less, it might receive 100% for this parameter, whereas a company with a EV/Sales ratio of 2.0 or more might receive 0%.

172 The formula is as follows: Attractiveness in % = (actual value – lowest value) / (highest value – lowest value), where the lowest value is the worst assumed result and the highest value is the best assumed result. For ratios that indicate attractiveness by lower values, the same formula applies, but it has to be subtracted from 1; i.e. attractiveness in % = 1 - (actual value – lowest value) / (highest value – lowest value).

By scaling all parameters, the results become comparable. It is now possible to say that the Debt/EBIT ratio of company X has an attractiveness score of Y%, whereas its PE indicates only Z% of attractiveness. To make it work, however, the user who inputs all ranges must have some understanding of the underlying parameters and the ability to assess their values in relation to buyout attractiveness.[173] In the subsequent section, a full application is demonstrated with value ranges for each parameter.

To finally arrive at a single output for buyout attractiveness, all scaled parameters must be weighted and then summed into one number. This number, between 0% and 100%, is the final score for buyout attractiveness given the model's assumptions. The weight given to each parameter can be freely chosen and changed at any time, thereby allowing a high degree of flexibility of the application. Furthermore, if data for a parameter is not available, or a parameter is not applicable for a specific company such as a negative PE, the model automatically adjusts the remaining weights. Moreover, a user can add 'kick-outs' to the model, so that companies that do not fulfill a certain 'kick-out' condition will automatically receive a zero final score. For instance, one 'kick-out' in the following application of the model is a market capitalization of EUR 15 million. Any company with a lower market capitalization will not be considered, even though all other parameters might indicate strong attractiveness.[174]

Technically speaking, most of the above listed parameters are easy to implement using common spreadsheet functions. The IRR, however, being the output of the LBO model, consists of several calculation layers.[175] To calculate the IRR for multiple companies at once within one or several spreadsheets would not be feasible.[176] Therefore, a simple macro in visual basic was developed that takes all

---

173 A helpful function of the model is its provision of average percentages of attractiveness for each parameter, once a range has been set.

174 More regarding the reasoning for this 'kick-out' in section 7.2.

175 As discussed, these are leverage, projections, and valuation.

176 The first reason is that MS Excel or the user's computer system might run into scalability issues. E.g. to derive the IRR for 2000 companies using the calculation steps of the LBO

companies through the LBO model and calculates the IRR for each.[177] This result, as well as the results of all other parameters, is then scaled and weighted to derive the final buyout attractiveness score. In the following, the companies can be ranked according to their score or any other parameters. The subsequent flow diagram visually summarizes the working of the extended model.

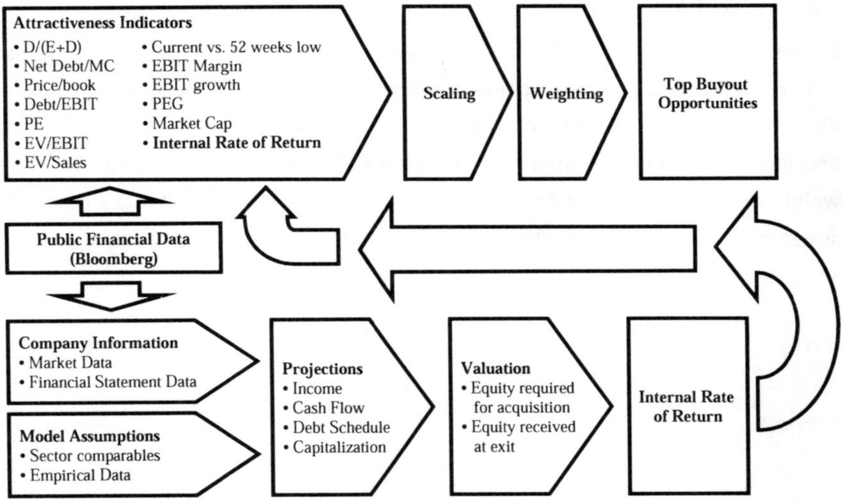

Figure 11: Extended model overview

A brief note on handling the extended model: All adjustments to the model can be made in the InputsLBO sheet (for the IRR calculation) or in the ScoringInputs sheet (all remaining parameters, scaling and weighting). New companies can easily be added and the data of existing companies can be straightforwardly

---

model would lead to a table with 2,000 * 5 (years) * 30 (lines) = 300,000 fields of formulas. More importantly, changes to the LBO model would be time consuming, error prone and difficult to understand, whereas the current version allows easy changes in the calculations or assumptions.

177 The source code of the macro belonging to the model can be viewed by starting the Microsoft Visual Basic Editor in the Tools menu of Microsoft Excel and then choosing the "Main" module.

updated.[178] The number of companies that can be analyzed with the model is limited only by the calculating power of Excel and the user's operating environment. Since all parameters are fully adjustable and instantly change the results, the model allows searches for companies with certain characteristics and can be attuned to the specific needs of the user.

7.2 Model Application

In the following, we apply the extended model to the European Technology markets with the aim of identifying potentially attractive buyout targets.[179] This also allows for a preliminary assessment on the quality of the results. As previously described, to apply the model we need to make decisions about the weight and scale of the model's parameters for attractiveness, values that were assigned as follows (next table):

---

[178] The spreadsheets are designed to utilize data sources such as Bloomberg, Datastream or Reuters. All company data can be loaded into the Bloomberg sheet from which it is used for the calculations. Appendix B contains detailed instructions on the use of the model.

[179] Other geographic markets would equally suit for an application of the model. The European markets were chosen for two reasons. First, high-profile technology buyout investors have traditionally focused their activities in the US, but some are increasingly looking to explore opportunities in Europe. The model might indicate whether opportunities exist that are worth pursuing. See also: Reed, Europe: Buyout Fever!, p. 60; Gilhuly, Private equity investors in the new European marketplace, p. 77. Second, the US market is already substantially more screened than the European market and might inhibit a higher degree of efficiency. Alongside this, the higher volatility of the European technology markets (e.g., compare NEMAX vs. NASDAQ) might offer additional opportunity for bargains.

Criteria	**Scale/Range**		**Direction**	**KickOuts**		**Weights**	**Group Weight**	
	Lowest 0	Highest 1	Best case Low (3)[180]	Min	Max			
Est. LBO IRR	0.1	0.5				46%	IRR	46%
D/(E+D)	0	1	3			1.5%		
Net Debt/MC	0	0.7	3			5.25%	Debt	12%
Price/book	0	3	3			1.25%		
Debt/EBIT	0	10	3			3.5%		
PE	1	25	3			3.5%		
EV/EBIT	1	15	3			9.5%	Valu-	29%
EV/Sales	0.05	2	3			13.25%	ation	
Current vs 52 weeks low	1	2	3			2.5%		
EBIT Margin	0	0.2				2.5%	Perform-	
EBIT growth	0	100				8.75%	ance &	14%
PEG	0	1.8	3			2.5%	other	
Market Cap				15				
Sum						100%		100%

Table 7: Applied weights and scales

The IRR naturally carries the most weight, followed by valuation multiples, performance figures and debt ratios. For valuation multiples, EV/Sales was given the highest weight (13.25%, range: 0.05 to 2) since it would apply to all companies independent of their profitability and was not included in the LBO model's terminal value derivation. Other heavily weighted parameters are EV/EBIT (9.5%), EBIT growth (8.75%), and Net Debt/MC (5.25%). Companies with a market capitalization of lower than EUR 15 million were excluded ('kicked-out'), since their value is too low to be of interest to private equity investors.[181] As a result, the chosen distribution of weights over the parameter groups looks as follows:

[180] A "3" in the "Direction" column is used to indicate when a lower value means higher attractiveness.

[181] Major technology buyout investors do rarely invest below EUR/USD 50 million equity. See: Silver Lake Partners, investment philosophy, w/o pg. Even for smaller players, EUR 15 million would be too lowly valued in most cases to be of interest.

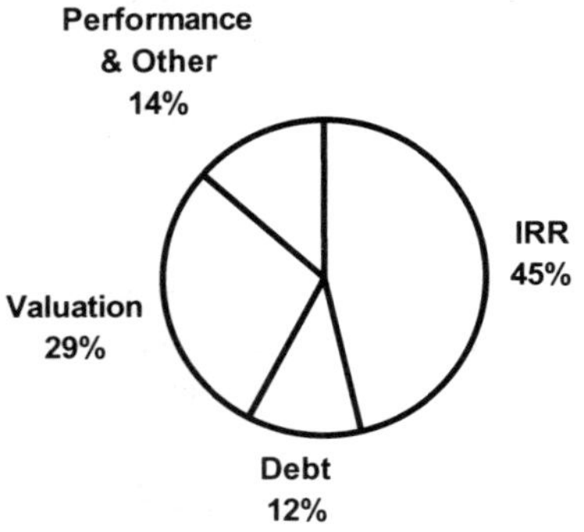

Figure 12: Parameter weightings

The data for the market screening was provided by Bloomberg, a major financial data information service, using end of day quotes from February 6, 2002. All financial statement data provided by Bloomberg is usually compiled from the most recent end-of-year reports. It should be noted that due to companies' different financial periods and reporting requirements, the financial statement data are not fully consistent. As will be further explained, the freshness and consistency of that data could be seen as a shortcoming of the model application.

The companies were chosen for the analysis by their membership in major European Technology Indices and selected small and mid-cap indices:

Selected European indices for the analysis[182]
CSFB EUROPEAN TECH
NASDAQ EUROPE COMPOSITE (EASDAQ)
FTSE TECHMARK ALL SHARE
FTSE AIM (ALTERNATIVE INVESTMENT MARKET)
NOUVEA MARCHE
NEMAX ALL SHARE
MDAX (DAX MIDCAP INDEX),
SMAX (DAX SMALLCAP INDEX)
SWX NEW MARKET

Table 8: Analyzed indices

182 The complete company list is viewable in the Bloomberg sheet of the excel file that contains the model (available for download at http://www.connect.to/techbuyouts - password: "leverage").

In total, more than 1,600 companies were part of the analysis of which approximately over half (800) can be regarded as technology companies in a more rigid form. 124 companies of those companies that were classified by Bloomberg as technology or communications companies had negative enterprise values (more cash on hand than market capitalization). This once more demonstrates the broad range of valuation to which technology companies are subject today. It also supports the model's attempt to include negatively valued companies in its analysis. The subsequent lists present the top 15 negatively valued companies in the technology and communications sectors as classified by Bloomberg. In aggregate, these companies alone have a negative enterprise value of over EUR 1 billion.[183] Although their effective value for investors is often not clear, some recent transactions suggest that negatively valued companies can provide plausible acquisition opportunities.[184]

Technology Industry

Rank	Company Name	MC	EV	Debt	Cash	Sales	EBIT	Net Inc.	N. Capex
1	RIVERSOFT PLC	37	-63	1	156	8	-43	-43	7
2	ARC INTERNATIONAL PLC	161	-45	1	4	17	-30	-27	5
3	ORCHESTREAM HOLDINGS	21	-37	1	95	4	-19	-17	2
4	KNOWLEDGE SUPPORT SYS.	16	-30	1	2	5	-6	-3	2
5	PATSYSTEMS PLC	19	-25	1	60	4	-16	-16	1
6	IVU TRAFFIC TECHNOLOGIES	18	-24	1	21	18	2	1	4
7	ACTIVCARD	286	-23	1	320	31	-16	-17	1
8	VALOR COMPUTERIZED SYS.	22	-21	1	4	32	3	4	1
9	THINK TOOLS AG	40	-17	7	19	17	7	-13	2
10	FFASTFILL PLC	3	-16	1	19	2	-9	-8	1
11	BOOKHAM TECHNOLOGY	285	-16	4	433	36	-62	-184	39
12	POET HOLDINGS INC	16	-15	1	20	13	-13	-11	n.a.
13	OPTIMS	9	-13	1	n.a.	22	2	0	n.a.
14	I:FAO AG	8	-13	n.a.	12	3	-12	-8	4
15	TELE ATLAS NV	85	-12	21	178	62	-9	-6	2

Table 9: Highest negative EV technology companies[185]

[183] The aggregated enterprise value of the listed 30 companies is EUR -1,024 million. However, as one underlying of this figure (the value of debt and cash) is based on the most recent financials and the other underlying is the current market value, the stated enterprise value is only an approximation. Material developments could have happened (e.g., the cash was spent), so that the actual enterprise value is higher than the reported one.

[184] For instance, CONCEPT! AG, a German IT services company that was listed at Neuer Markt with a negative enterprise value of over EUR 50 million (MC: 39.9; EV: -54.8; 26.07.2001; source: Bloomberg) was acquired by a UK strategic buyer for an announced premium of 51% on January 16, 2002 (Source: Mergerstat/Bloomberg).

[185] All figures in million EUR except multiples. Data compiled from Bloomberg, 06.02.2002.

Communications Industry									
Rank	Company Name	MC	EV	Debt	Cash	Sales	EBIT	Net Inc.	N. Capex
1	LYCOS EUROPE N.V.	213	-115	1	353	139	-1,124	-1,002	n.a.
2	GAMEPLAY PLC	2	-76	2	78	n.a.	-58	-321	-2
3	IZODIA PLC	28	-70	n.a.	151	4	-81	-59	2
4	EMBLAZE SYSTEMS LIMITED	277	-51	n.a.	311	50	-6	19	3
5	FANTASTIC CORP	38	-49	2	78	19	-61	-65	3
6	REDBUS INTERHOUSE PLC	19	-45	2	139	6	-12	-87	23
7	MEDIASCAPE COM.	16	-34	1	12	4	-6	-3	6
8	AD PEPPER MEDIA NV	14	-32	n.a.	5	15	-12	-10	1
9	LYCOS France	21	-31	n.a.	5	4	-18	-21	1
10	EARTHPORT PLC	5	-28	2	34	1	-18	-38	0
11	DCI DATABASE	11	-27	n.a.	39	12	-22	-22	n.a.
12	ACTINIC PLC	7	-26	n.a.	34	2	-5	-11	0
13	TEAMTALK MEDIA GROUP	19	-25	1	44	16	-17	-25	5
14	NETVALUE	12	-23	1	6	3	-25	-21	3
15	TRAVEL24.COM	11	-21	2	34	26	-25	-34	3

Table 10: Highest negative EV communications companies[186]

7.1 Top European Technology Buyout Candidates

Following is a table listing the highest scoring buyout opportunities when the extended model is applied to the selected indices, given the chosen parameter weights and ranges and given the assumptions of the LBO model. To ease the analysis, the listing includes only companies classified by Bloomberg as being in the technology or communications industry. A broader definition of technology in the sense of the discussion in section 3.1 would allow the inclusion of substantially more companies. Media companies, being part of the communications industry as classified by Bloomberg, also were excluded.

A cross check was conducted to also exclude companies that experienced materially negative financial developments following their latest reported financial year results and whose latest annual report would be a questionable indicator of the company's current financial situation.[187] The latter analysis, however, was done only on a preliminary basis and some of the data presented might still be significantly different from the present situation.[188]

---

186 All figures in million EUR except multiples. Data compiled from Bloomberg, 06.02.2002.

187 The footnote of the subsequent table presenting the identified top buyout opportunities contains a list of the excluded companies.

188 E.g., EBIT of Ruecker AG is not in line with the announced nine months results (adjusted; source: company website). However, some numbers are also understated: Think Tools AG's

Overall, due to the historic nature of the data used and the restrictions set by the model, the listed companies do not necessarily represent sound buyout opportunities solely on the basis of this analysis. Obviously, a more thorough analysis of the individual company would have to be conducted to determine its actual buyout attractiveness. The data do present a useful benchmark for the initial evaluation, however.

Score	Company Name	IRR	PE	EV/EBIT	EV/Sales	MC	EV	Debt	Cash	Sales	EBIT
74%	RUECKER AG	40%	8	2.3	0.3	42	29	18	32	115	12
73%	EASY SOFTWARE	43%	5	4.3	0.4	15	18	5	2	41	4
71%	AVENIR TELECOM	32%	n/a	0.7	0.0	121	36	31	118	1,111	53
68%	TRIA IT-SOLUTIONS	33%	33	4.4	0.5	18	15	1	5	30	3
68%	COMINO GROUP	35%	7	3.8	0.5	25	18	1	13	35	5
67%	PARITY GROUP PLC	36%	7	4.4	0.2	95	95	11	7	438	21
63%	CEYONIQ AG	37%	7	7.1	2.5	132	187	39	12	74	26
62%	THINK TOOLS AG	32%	n/a	n/a	n/a	40	-17	7	19	17	7
58%	SOFTWARE AG-REG	31%	12	6.6	1.8	792	754	3	155	417	114
56%	IB GROUP.COM	29%	9	4.7	0.4	32	42	21	12	120	9
52%	RM PLC	23%	7	3.4	0.2	124	81	3	34	393	24
51%	LINX PRINTING	25%	11	7.9	0.9	65	70	6	1	77	9
51%	AZLAN GROUP PLC	19%	13	8.7	0.2	246	237	16	12	962	27
50%	MACRO 4 PLC	29%	20	5.8	0.9	65	72	20	14	77	12
50%	TRACING SERVER	21%	15	9.2	0.9	23	24	2	1	26	3
49%	DELCAM PLC	22%	9	8.0	0.7	17	18	3	1	28	2
49%	SHERWOOD INTER.	26%	10	6.5	0.9	93	78	1	31	88	12
47%	DATA MODUL AG	21%	16	9.1	0.5	40	53	16	2	111	6
47%	TA TRIUMPH-ADLER	30%	18	7.1	0.6	135	419	281	14	719	59
45%	ELMOS SEMICOND.	26%	13	8.1	2.0	222	231	35	74	116	29

Table 11: Top 20 European tech buyout opporunities given model assumptions and Bloomberg historical data[189]

What are the patterns of the listed top buyout opportunities? A broad range of intra-industry sectors is represented, from enterprise software, IT services, document management, and telecom equipment, over to technology engineering

cash position as reported by Bloomberg significantly differs from the last reported figure by the company of CHF 87.3 million (07.08.2001; source: company website).

189 All financials are in million EUR except multiples. Data from Bloomberg, technology and communications industry only, 06.02.2002, end of day quotes; UK financials converted at currency rates of 7/2/2002: 1.00 GB = 1.62524 EUR. List excludes media companies and companies with significant changes in currently available interim financials compared to the most recent financial year figures used by Bloomberg (preliminary analysis). The companies excluded for the latter reason are: Dataflex Holding plc, Icos Vision Systems NV, Kudelski SA-Bearer, IVU Traffic Technologies AG, Flomerics Group plc., ASM International, Topcall International, Touchstone Group plc, Plasmon plc, Comroad AG.

services. No one country dominates the list, though the UK and Germany lead and are followed by France. A general characteristic of the listed companies is their low relative valuation (Average EV/Sales: 0.8; EV/EBIT: 6.1). Additionally, all have significant EBITs that would potentially allow acquirers to finance a deal in part with debt capital (the average EBIT margin is 12%). Despite the currently difficult economic conditions, some of the companies have highly positive operating developments with strong sales and earnings growth that are not yet reflected in the data used.[190]

7.2 Findings and Interpretation

To interpret the quality of the results, we must distinguish two determinants: the quality of the data and the quality of the model itself. The model can only produce results as good as the data put in to it. Assuming the quality of data is good and fairly represents the actual financial situation of each company, the model's results can be seen as fully in line with characteristics of attractive targets: Low valuation, substantial cash flows (as indicated by their EBIT), and low existing leverage. Moreover, the estimation of the IRR provides a way of relating a company's cash flows to its current valuation and debt capacity and thereby allows for more meaningful results than pure ratio-based analysis. It can actually estimate what returns investors could generate by buying out a specific company and therefore can approximate the results of an LBO investor's analysis performed before an actual buyout takes place. Overall, the model appears to have produced the results desired: The recognition of companies that can be considered as highly attractive buyout targets given the provided data.

The quality of the data used was sufficient for a preliminary screening. Although historical data was used, the resulting short list of companies does represent companies that might be viewed as attractive buyout opportunities. Without basing this on further analysis, companies such as RM plc, TA Triumph Adler AG and Software AG may provide interesting buyout opportunities for financial

---

190 E.g. TA Triumph Adler AG posted an increase in sales for the first nine months 2001 of 30%; Ruecker increased sales during the same period 21%, while Software AG grew their full year sales for 2001 41% (Source: company websites).

investors.[191] Although final attractiveness can only be declared ex-post (once a company has indeed been bought out and returns have been made), the financials of these companies and currently prevailing market conditions suggest that opportunities exist for technology buyouts in Europe. Out of the whole set of 1,600 companies, 47 or 2.9% had IRRs over 20%, confirming that there are potential buyout targets in the screened market.

Although both data and the rigid assumptions of the model serve sufficiently well, there are ways for further improvement. Since the current market capitalization of a company includes today's best knowledge of its future development, whereas the data used to project the future development in the model application was taken from financial statements possibly as old as a year, an advanced version of the model would aim to synchronize the projections with future expectations. An elegant and technically feasible way of doing this would involve basing the projections on analyst estimates and using analyst consensus figures to project sales and EBIT for each company over the buyout horizon.[192] A practical problem in doing so, however, would be the sometimes sparse or outdated coverage of smaller technology stocks. Furthermore, some studies suggest that the quality of analyst forecasting is not always superior to historical estimates. Additionally, substantial parts of the investment community question their ability in general following the market downturn in 2000.[193] Nevertheless, an application of the model based on analyst estimates likely would add additional meaning to the results.

---

[191] An individual company analysis for buyout attractiveness is not part of this study. As mentioned, all companies would need to be individually analysed to determine further buyout suitability. The results only indicate preliminary attractiveness as a basis for further evaluation.

[192] Using information services such as I/B/E/S, now a part of First Call, analyst consensus estimates could be linked directly into an Excel spreadsheet, similar to the Bloomberg API (Application Programming Interface) used.

[193] Especially for long-term forecasts, analyst projections do not seem to outperform statistical methods. See: Crichfield/Dyckman/Lakonishok, An evaluation of security analyst's forecasts, pp. 667; O'Brien, Analysts' forecasts as earnings expectations, p. 82.

7.3 Suggestions for Further Research

Based on our findings from the model application and on previous reflections on the characteristics of technology buyouts, the following briefly summarizes areas in which further research would be of value to the understanding of technology buyouts:

- Statistical and empirical analysis is needed on average expected rates of return, leverage ratios, management participation, acquisition premiums, and country comparisons. In particular, the question of a technology risk premium, which would be indicated by higher required rates of return, would provide valuable insight into practical valuation efforts of technology buyouts.

- Advancement in applications that allow for analytical screening of markets would increase market transparency and provide valuable information to both investors and companies. Although the degree of precision is ultimately limited by standardized models, the incorporation of analyst projections and more sophisticated algorithms could improve their results.

- Finally, empirical, meaningful evidence on technology buyout performance would be of considerable value. Various conclusions might be drawn, such as a benchmarking with traditional buyouts. The relatively small number of past transactions as well as the long investment cycles for buyouts should make this only a medium and long-term goal.

8 Summary and Conclusion

Our key findings can be summarized as follows:

- Based on past transactions, raised funds, and general economic and industrial developments, we concluded that the concept of technology buyouts has a certain degree of substance, being more than a short-term or over-hyped investment idea. We found that technology buyouts inhibit greater risks, but also provide more upside in the form of growth than traditional buyouts.

- We identified the Equity Cash Flow method to be a well-working valuation approach for buyout situations, and therefore incorporated it into a spreadsheet model that provides as outcome the internal rate of return to investors. The idea was to estimate returns with only publicly available data as input. For that, we drew on a set of assumptions, of which constant sales growth, constant EBIT margin, and the same exit multiple as entrance multiple were the most important.

- We discussed a number of ways to account for technology-specific risk and return characteristics. Identified were an adjustment of the required rate of return, capital expenditure ratios and, most practically, cash flow projections. We noted the theoretical inconsistencies of arbitrary return rate adjustments with asset pricing models, as well as the problems of value additions based on real options.

- Finally, we extended the model to incorporate other parameters that might have been neglected or that provide added meaning to the results. The outcome is a spreadsheet model that allows the user to specify his or her desired target characteristics and screen stock markets in a convenient and flexible way. When we used market and historical financial statement data from over 1,600 companies in European growth and technology indices, we identified a small but significant number of companies that would be suitable as potential buyout targets. This result led us to conclude that the stock market downturn since mid-2000 may have created technology buyout opportunities in Europe.

During the time this thesis was being written, more European technology companies were bought out and taken private. In January 2002, the banking software subsidiary of German Neuer Markt-listed SER Systems AG was acquired by an investor group (led by CornerstoneCapital and Heptagon Capital) and management. A few weeks after, traditional UK buyout firm Alchemy Partners bought out enterprise software maker Cedar Group plc for GBP 42.5 million.[194] Probably the most notable buyout thus far has been the EUR 1.7 billion acquisition of various divisions, including the network systems group, of Siemens by KKR in July 2002.[195] These and other examples demonstrate that Europe, with the existence of large technology conglomerates as well as its volatile growth markets, continues to emerge as an interesting playing field for technology buyout investors.

[194] Jaffe, Tough times for VCs to play power tripage, w/o pg.

[195] However, not all businesses acquired from Siemens by KKR can be regarded technology in a more rigid form. Major part of the transaction included the traditional machinery companies formerly belonging to Atecs Mannesmann, as well as businesses of Siemens' power generation and transmission group. See: Kohlberg Kravis Roberts & Co. (Ed.), KKR acquires 7 businesses from Siemens AG, w/o pg.

References

Altman, Edward I./Hukkawala, Naeem/Kishore, Vellore: *Defaults and Returns on High-Yield Bonds: Lessons from 1999 and Outlook for 2000-2002*, in: Business Economics, vol. 35, issue 2, 2000, pp. 27-39.

Altman, Edward I.: *Measuring corporate bond mortality and performance*, in: Journal of Finance, vol. 44, issue 4, 1989, pp. 909-922.

Andrade, Gregor/Gilson, Stuart/Pulvino, Todd: *Seagate Technology Buyout*, Harvard Business School Case 9-201-063, Boston 2001.

Andrade, Gregor/Kaplan, Steven: *How costly is financial distress? Evidence from highly leveraged transactions that became distressed*, 2000, http://papers.ssrn.com/sol3/papers.cfm?abstract_id29359, publication date: n.a., access date: 27.01.2002.

Anslinger, Patricia L./Copeland, Thomas E.: *Growth through acquisitions: A fresh look*, in: Harvard Business Review, no. 74, January-February 1996, pp. 126-135.

Asset Alternatives (Ed.), *Strategies for successful buyout investing*, http://www.assetnews.com/downloads/pub/buyout_charts.pdf, publication date: 2001, access date: 01.02.2002.

Auletta, Ken: *Greed and Glory on Wall Street: The fall of the house of Lehman*, New York 1986.

Baldwin, Carliss: *Technical note on LBO valuation (A)*, Harvard Business School Case 9-902-004, Boston 2001.

Bannock, Graham/Manser, William: *The Penguin international dictionary of finance*, London 1995.

Barry, David G./Dube, Michael R./Galante, Steven P.: *As technology industry matures, firms see buyout opportunities*, in: Asset Alternatives Online, Private Equity Update, http://www.assetnews.com/ped/techfund.htm, publication date: n.a., access date: 01.02.2002.

Baruch, Yehuda: *High technology organization – what it is, what it isn't*, in: International Journal of Technology Management, vol. 13, issue 2, 1997, pp. 179-195.

Benninga, Simon Z./Oded H. Sarig: *Corporate finance: a valuation approach*, New York 1997.

Benninga, Simon: *Financial Modeling*, London 2000.

Bernier, Paula: *Warren Buffet, Others Invest in Level 3*, in: XCHANGE Online, http://www.xchangemag.com/hotnews/27h810122.html, publication date: 08.07.2002, access date: 15.07.2002.

Black, Fischer/Scholes, Myron: *The valuation of option contracts and a test of market efficiency*, in: Journal of Finance, vol. 27, issue 2, 1972, pp. 399-417.

Bodie, Zvi/Kane, Alex/Marcus, Alan J.: *Investments*, 4th ed., New York 1999.

Boer, Peter F.: *The valuation of technology*, New York 1999.

Borio, Carlo E.: *Banks' involvement in highly leveraged transactions*, in: Bank for International Settlements (BIS) Economic Papers, no. 28, October 1990.

Brealey, Richard A/Myers, Steward C.: *Principles of corporate finance*, 6th, international ed., New York 2000.

Brown, Ken: *Some cheap firms still don't seem to find any takers*, in: The Wall Street Journal Europe, 25.04.2001, p. 16.

Bruck, Connie: *The predator's ball: The junk-bond raiders and the man who staked them*, New York 1988.

Bruner, Robert F.: *Leveraged ESOPs and corporate restructuring*, in: Journal of Applied Corporate Finance, issue 1, Spring 1988, pp. 54-66.

Brush, John S.: *Optimal sector models differ*, in: Pensions & Investments, vol. 29, issue 6, 2001, pp. 38-42.

Burrough, Bryan/Helyar, John: *Barbarians at the gate: The fall of RJR Nabisco*, New York 1990.

Christensen, Clayton M.: *The innovator's dilemma: when new technologies cause great firms to fail*, Boston 1997.

Copeland, Tom/Antikarov, Vladimir: *Real options: a practitioner's guide*, New York 2001.

Copeland, Tom/Koller, Tim/Murrin, Jack: *Valuation: measuring and managing the value of companies*, New York 1996.

Cricheld, Timothy/Dyckman, Thomas/Lakonishok, Joseph: *An evaluation of security analyst's forecasts*, in: Accounting Review, vol. 53, issue 3, 1978, pp. 651-667.

Damodaran, Aswath: *Corporate finance: Theory and practice*, 2nd ed., New York 1997.

Damodaran, Aswath: *The Dark Side of Valuation: Valuing Old Tech, New Tech and New Economy Companies*, New York 2001.

DeAngelo H./DeAngleo L./Rice E.: *Going private: The effects of a change in corporate ownership structure,* in: Midland Corporate Finance Journal, Summer 1984, pp. 35-43.

Deb, Dipanjan/Kesavan, Vasan: *A not-so-new idea for a not-so-new economy*, in: Siliconindia, vol. 5, issue 1, 2001, p. 74-77.

Dresdner Kleinwort Wasserstein (Ed.): *German Neuer Markt: The price of growth*, Frankfurt a. M. 2001.

Evans, Jim: *Leveraged buyout firms go tech*, in: Upside Today, http://www.upside.com/texis/mvm/print-it?id=34712clfle&t=, publication date: 10.11.1997, access date: 01.02.2002.

Fama, Eugene F./ French, Kenneth R.: *The cross section of expected stock returns*, in: Journal of Finance, vol. 47, issue 2, 1992, pp. 427-466.

Fox, Isaac/Marcus, Alfred: *The causes and consequences of leveraged management buyouts*, in: Academy of Management Review, vol. 17, issue 1, 1992, pp. 62-85.

Gallo, David: *Francisco Partners*, Harvard Business School Case 9-200-063, Boston 2000.

Gilhuly, Edward A.: *Private equity investors in the new European marketplace*, in: US-German Economic Yearbook 1999, New York 1999, pp. 76-81.

Gores Technology Group (Ed.): *The company*, http://www.gores.com/the company.html, publication date: n.a., access date: 28.01.2002.

Gove, Alex: *Raiding the valley*, in: Red Herring Magazine, issue 68, July 1999, http://www.redherring.com/mag/issue68/inv-lbo.html, publication date: 01.07.1999, access date: 01.02.2002.

Harvey, Campbell R.: *Hypertextual finance glossary*, http://www.duke.edu/~charvey/Classes/wpg/glossary.htm, publication date: n.a., access date: 01.02.2002.

Haugen, Carla: *Buyouts as an investment opportunity*, BARRA RogersCasey, 1999, http://www.barrarogerscasey.com/Data/Buyouts.pdf, publication date: 1999, access date: 01.02.2002.

Houghton Mifflin Company (Ed.): *The American Heritage Concise Dictionary*, 3rd ed., 1994.

Hull, John: *Options, futures, & other derivatives*, New York 2000.

Inselbag, Isik/Kaufold, Howard: *How to value recapitalizations and leveraged buyouts*, in: Journal of Applied Corporate Finance, vol. 2, issue 2, 1989, pp. 87-96.

Inselbag, Isik/Kaufold, Howard: *Valuation approaches to the LBO*, in: The Complete Finance Companion, Financial Times Mastering Series, London 1998, pp. 24-30.

Jaffe, Joshua: *Tough times force VCs to play power triage*, in: The Deal, http://208.185.43.170/NASApp/cs/ContentServer?pagename=TheDeal/TDDArticle/StandardArticle&c=TDDArticle&cid=1014044394638, publication date: 20.02.2002, access date: 20.02.2002.

Jensen, Micheal C./Chew, Donald H.: *US corporate governance: Lessons from the 1980s*, in: The Portable MBA in Finance and Accounting, New York 1995, pp. 337-404.

Jensen, Micheal C.: *Agency costs of free cash flow, corporate finance and takeovers*, in: American Economic Review, vol. 76, issue 2, 1986, pp. 323-330.

Kaplan, Steven N./Ruback, Richard S.: *The valuation of cash flow forecasts: An empirical analysis*, in: Journal of Finance, vol. 50, issue 4, 1995, pp. 1059-1094.

Kaplan, Steven N.: *Management buyouts: evidence on taxes as a source of value*, in: Journal of Finance, vol. 44, issue 3, 1998, pp. 611-632.

Kaplan, Steven N.: *The effects of management buyouts on operating performance and value*, in: Journal of Financial Economics, vol. 24, 1989, pp. 217-254.

Kaplan, Steven N.: *The staying power of leveraged buyouts,* in: Journal of Financial Economics, vol. 29, 1991, pp. 287-313.

Kester, Carl W./Luehrman, Timothy A.: *Rehabilitating the leveraged buyout*, in: Harvard Business Review, vol. 73, issue 3, 1995, pp. 119-131.

Kohlberg Kravis Roberts & Co. (Ed.): *Kohlberg Kravis Roberts & Co. L.P. and GS Capital Partners have agreed to acquire Siemens Nixdorf, soon to be re-named "Wincor Nixdorf"*, http://www.kkr.com/press/10_22_99.html, publication date: 22.10.1999, access date: 01.02.2002.

Kohlberg Kravis Roberts & Co. (Ed.): *KKR acquires 7 businesses from Siemens AG*, http://www.kkr.com/press/07_26_02.html, publication date: 26.07.2002, access date: 28.07.2002.

Lashinsky, Adam: *Five secrets of a turnaround ace*, in: Business 2.0, February 2002, http://www.business2.com/articles/mag/print/0,1643,36744,FF.html, publication date: January 2002, access date: 01.02.2002.

Leimbach, Andreas: *Transactions in corporate control: an empirical investigation of the nature, determinants and effects of corporate buyouts*, Frankfurt a. M. 1989.

Lenatti, Chuck: *Targeting tech for leveraged buyouts*, in: Upside Today, http://www.upside.com/texis/mvm/print-it?id=37fe66f80&t=1, publication date: 11.10.1999, access date: 01.02.2002.

Lerner, Joshua: *Venture capital and private equity: A casebook*, New York 2000.

Lewis, Michael: *Liar's Poker: Rising through the wreckage on Wall Street*, London/New York 1989.

Li, Ling Hin: *Simple computer applications improve the versatility of discounted cash flow analysis*, in: The Appraisal Journal, vol. 68, issue 1, 2000, pp. 86-92.

Lintener, John: *The valuation of risk assets, and the selections of risky investments in stock portfolios and capital budgets*, in: Review of Economics and Statistics, vol. 47, issue 1, pp. 13-37.

Loihl, Angela K.: *Buyouts in the technology sector*, Nottingham 2000.

MacDonald, Elizabeth: *PeopleShell?*, in: Forbes Magazine, February 2002, pp. 93-94.

Miles, James A./Ezzel, John R.: *The weighted average cost of capital, perfect capital markets, and project life: a clarification*, in: Journal of Financial and Quantitative Analysis, vol. 15, issue 3, 1980, pp. 719-730.

Miller, Merton/Modigliani, Franco: *Dividend policy, growth, and the valuation of shares?*, in: Journal of Business, vol. 34, issue 4, 1961, pp. 411-433.

Miller, Tim: *Buyer finding gold in tech wrecks*, in: M&A Insider, vol. 7, issue 1, Spring 2001, pp. 1, 3.

Moriarty, George: *Convergent, MSDW eye buyouts in tech sector*, in: Buyouts, http://www.findarticles.com/cf_dls/m0UGQ/1999_April_5/54306998./print.jhtml, publication date: 05.04.1999, access date: 01.02.2002.

Mossin, Jan: *Equilibrium in a capital asset market*, in: Econometrica, vol. 34, 1966, pp. 768-783.

Myers, Steward C.: *Interactions of corporate financing and investment decisions – implications for capital budgeting*, in: Journal of Finance, vol. 29, issue 1, 1974, pp. 1-25.

Nygard, Wayne/Razaire, Christophe: *Probability-based DCF: an alternative to point-value estimates*, in: The Appraisal Journal, vol. 67, issue 1, 1999, pp. 68-74.

O'Brien, Patricia C.: *Analysts' forecasts as earnings expectations,* in: Journal of Accounting and Economics, vol. 10, issue 1, 1988, pp. 53-83.

Partnoy, Frank: *F.I.A.S.C.O.: Blood in the water on Wall Street*, New York 1997.

Pratt, Shannon P.: *Business valuation: discounts and premiums*, New York 2001.

Rabinovitz, Jonathan: *Leveraged buyouts' strange return*, in: The Industry Standard, issue January 10-17, 2000, http://www.thestandard.com/article/0,1902,8458,00.html, publication date: 10.01.2000, access date: 01.02.2002.

RCW Mirus (Ed.): *Management buyouts*, http://www.merger.com/upload/spot_pdf/spotlight_mbofuture.pdf, publication date: 03.2001, access date: 01.02.2002.

Reed, Stanley: *Europe: Buyout Fever!*, in: Business Week, international ed., issue 3636, June 14, 1999, pp. 60-61.

Richerstein, Rick: *Buyout*, New York 2001.

Robb, Russel: *Acquisition financing in today's volatile marketplace*, in: M&A Insider, vol. 7, issue 1, Spring 2001, pp. 1, 3.

Robbie, Ken/Wright, Mike/Albrighton, Mark: *High-tech management buyouts*, in: Venture Capital, vol. 1, issue 3, 1999, pp. 219-239.

Ross, Stephen/Westerfield, Randolph/Jordan, Jeffrey: *Corporate finance*, 5th ed., Burr Ridge 1998.

Schack, Justin: *LBOverload?*, in: Institutional Investor, vol. 35, issue 6, 2001, pp. 28-29.

Schwartz, Eduardo/Moon, Mark: *Rational pricing of Internet companies*, in: Financial Analysts Journal, vol. 56, issue 3, 2000, pp. 62-75.

Silver Lake Partners (Ed.): *Investment philosophy*, http://www.slpartners.com/focus.html, publication date: n.a., access date: 01.02.2002.

Smith, Abbie: *Corporate ownership structure and performance,* in: Journal of Financial Economics, vol. 27, 1990, pp. 143-164.

Stewart, James Brewer: *Den of the Thieves*, New York 1991.

Taylor, George: *The emergence of technology buyouts*, Harvard Business School paper, Boston 2000, unpublished.

The Deal (Ed.): *Average premiums: European targets – February 7, 2002*, in: The Deal, http://www.thedeal.com/NASApp/cs/ContentServer?pagename =TheDeal/TDDArticle/StandardArticle&c=TDDArticle&cid=1013038807 031, publication date: 07.02.2002, access date: 09.02.2002.

The Deal (Ed.): *M&A acquirer advisory fees - February 21, 2002*, in: The Deal, http://www.thedeal.com/NASApp/cs/ContentServer?pagename=TheDeal/ TDDArticle/ StandardArticle&c=TDDArticle&cid=1014044391558, publication date: 21.02.2002, access date: 21.02.2002.

Thomas, Russell: *Business value analysis: - coping with unruly uncertainty*, in: Strategy & Leadership, vol. 29, issue 2, 2001, pp. 16-20.

Vicente, J. P.: *Anatomy of an LBO*, in: Red Herring Magazine, issue 87, December 2000, http://www.redherring.com/mag/issue87/mag-anatomy-87.html, publication date: 01.12.2000, access date: 01.02.2002.

Vicente, J. P.: *Private matters,* in: Red Herring Magazine, issue 87, December 2000, http://www.redherring.com/mag/issue87/mag-matters-87.html, publication date: 01.12.2000, access date: 01.02.2002.

W/o a.: *German institutions keen on private equity*, in: Private Equity Online, http://www.privateequityonline.com/dealfocus.asp?id=2254, publication date: 23.01.2002, access date: 01.02.2002.

Wade, Will: *New equity fund shopping in tech market with $700M*, in: EETimes Online, http://www.eetimes.com/story/OEG20010314S0051, publication date: 14.03.2001, access date: 01.02.2002.

Webb, Ian: *Management buy-outs*, Hants 1990.

Weston, Fred J./Siu, Juan A./Johnson, Brian A.: *Takeovers, restructuring & corporate governance*, 3rd ed., Upper Saddle River (New York) 2001.

William Sharp: *Capital asset prices: a theory of market equilibrium*, in: Journal of Finance, vol. 19, issue 3, 1964, pp. 425-442.

Wright, Mike/Burrows, Andrew/Loihl, Angela: *Technology sector buyouts*, in: European Venture Capital Journal, December-January 2001, pp. 12-15.

Wright, Mike/Thompson, Steve/Robbie, Ken: *Venture capital and management-led, leveraged buy-outs: A European perspective*, in: Journal of Business Venturing, vol. 7, issue 1, 1992, pp. 47-71.

Wright, Mike: *Entrepreneurial growth through privatisation*, in: Academy of Management Review, vol. 25, issue 3, 2000, pp. 591-602.

List of Appendixes

Appendix A: Field Description Sheet

Cash-out Horizon in years	The cash-out horizon is assumed to be a constant. If it is changed, the projection and valuation sheets must be extended or shortened. Assumptions about constant cash-out horizons are common practice and necessary to make the model work. Empirical data of LBO investment durations indicate that 3-7 years with five years being the mean is a well working assumption. Note that the cash-out horizon has significant impact on the IRR due to the annual compounding effect.
Management Participation (%)	The management participation in % measures the assumed contribution of the buyout management team to the equity. Depending on the size of the deal, it can go from a few percentile to close to the majority. For publicly listed firms 5% -10% can be considered as a working average.
Management Discount (%)	Usually the management is able to participate in a buyout deal at a discount or with special financing comparable to a discount. The field measures how much less in % the management pays per share than the buyout fund.
Required cash on hand in % of sales	Every company needs to maintain liquidity. This assumption field records how much cash the company should keep throughout the buyout horizon in % of sales.
Cash Account 2001	Cash and marketable securities at the year stated as base year.
Proceeds from Asset Sale	This field only appears for individual company analysis when assumptions about asset sale proceeds following the buyout can be made. All proceeds from asset sales are assumed to pay off any remaining debt and to be reinvested leading to sales growth at the net Capex / sales growth rate, which is input separately. This method was chosen since a direct deduction of asset sales from buyer's equity in the base year would in some cases lead to negative equity paid. Moreover, timing and amount of proceeds from asset sales cannot be projected with certainty.
Pre-acquisition Debt	The outstanding debt of the target prior to any buyout (note: not the net debt). The pre-acquisition debt will be fully assumed and carried over.
Long-term government bond rate	The effective annual yield on the long-term government bond of the country/region of the targets. For targets in Europe, the 10-year bund (German government bond) and for targets in the US the 10 year government bond are commonly used.
EBIT Coverage Ratio 2002	The EBIT interest coverage ratio is a key driver for the creditworthiness and therefore the rating of a company. It measures to what extent the annual interest payments of the firm are covered by its operating income. E.g. a coverage ratio of three means that the company generates or is expected to generate operating income of three times its interest payments. Worksheet LeverageLBO contains a table showing the linkage between coverage ratio and rating. Note that the ratio increases as debt is being paid down over the buyout horizon. (see ValuationLBO worksheet for each year's interest coverage ratio)

Rating The field shows the rating of the company given the entered interest coverage ratio. Depending on credit market conditions, companies going through leveraged buyouts must maintain a certain rating to access debt capital. Furthermore, ratings significantly below investment grade carry prohibitive debt capital costs, making future capital raising difficult.

Maximum interest expense This is the maximum amount of interest that the company can pay given the expected next-year EBIT and a desired interest coverage ratio.

Cost of Debt The estimated cost of debt results from adding the corporate spread determined by the company rating and the government bond rate. Note that corporate spreads change over time and also depend on the individual company and sector. The table provided in the LeverageLBO worksheet linking ratings to corporate spreads serves as a working approximation.

Debt Capacity Given the estimated cost of debt and interest expenses, this field indicates how much debt the firm would be able to assume.

Pre-acquisition Net-Debt The net-debt pre-acquisition equals the market value of outstanding debt minus the cash account. If the firm owns more cash or marketable securities than it has outstanding debt, the net-debt is negative and can also be referred to as net cash.

Enterprise Value It was Modigliani and Miller who in their first proposition of finance put forward that the enterprise value (or Fundamental Market Value) of a company equals its value of (net) debt and its value of equity. Therefore, the enterprise value is calculated as market capitalization minus net debt. Note that minority value is ignored as it is assumed to be not material.

EV/EBIT The Enterprise/EBIT multiple of the base year, pre-acquisition has strong impact as it serves as the exit multiple of the model and therefore determines the exit equity value. It is assumed that the entrance and exit multiples are equal.

EV/Sales For information purposes, the EV/Sales provides some indication of the current market valuation relative to the firm's sales.

Exit P/E The P/E multiple states the price/earnings ratio of the estimated exit value. It can be used to double-check the soundness of the analysis.

Sales 2001 This is the sales figure of the base year, which is the basis for the sales projections of the subsequent years.

EBIT 2001 The earnings before interest and tax (EBIT) figure of the base year. This number is a core driver of the model as the future projections keep the margin of the base year. Although margins are in reality not constant and might in fact increase following a buyout and are subject to changing market conditions, this seems to be a reasonable approach, particularly as EBIT should mostly be free of one-time items (in opposition to net income). Two alternative routes: 1.) Estimate an industry margin and enter the appropriate EBIT figure at this margin. 2.) Instead of constant growth and constant margins, use analyst expectations of EBIT (and sales etc) as projections.

Sales growth rate of excess cash If a company has excess cash at the beginning (e.g., a negative enterprise value or proceeds from asset sales) or during the buyout horizon and has already repaid all debt, this excess cash will be reinvested in the company operations. The result will be an increase in sales of the assumed "sales growth rate of excess cash". E.g. if the sales growth rate is 2, excess cash of 100 will result in increased sales in the next year of 200.

Average sales growth Another core driver of the model, the estimated sales growth, is the annual growth rate in revenues over the buyout horizon. It can either be estimated using comparable sector data or fundamental research. Alternatively, as for the EBIT, analyst estimates could be used for the sales projections.

Corporate tax rate The standard corporate tax rate of the country in question. Note that no other taxes or tax-deductible items are taken into account other than the tax shield of debt.

Net Capital Expenditures / sales growth The net-capital expenditures to sales growth ratio is a key model driver. Its value measures what percentage of sales growth between the current and previous year has to be spent as net capital expenditures (the capital expenditures above depreciation). High growth comes (in most cases) from capital investments, and therefore a higher estimated sales growth rate is to be financed by higher capital expenditures.

Increase in NWC / sales growth Similar to the net-capital expenditures / sales growth ratio, the net working capital to sales growth ratio describes the increase of net working capital as a percentage of sales growth from the previous to the current year. As with the net capital expenditures, the increase in net working capital is to be reduced from the operating income to arrive at the cash flow available to share- and debt holders.

Market Capitalization The market capitalization measures the value of the equity of the firm. (For companies with very low free float or voting share separation, this might, however, sometimes not reflect the fair value of the firm's equity.)

Transaction Costs / Acquisition Price Usually, transaction costs occur as percentage of the overall transaction sum. Depending on company size and complexity of the transaction, an overall fee for professional service providers (investment banks, accountants, lawyers, trading fees in some cases, etc.) in the range of 2% - 5% can be estimated.

Amortization of Transaction Costs in years	Pending further accounting regulations, transaction costs are accounted as amortization over specified periods of time according to the country's tax and accounting rules. As transaction costs are amortized but paid at the time of the acquisition by the equity investors, they have to be added to the operating income in order to arrive at free cash flows. The field input of the duration of transaction cost amortization should in most cases be the horizon of the investment.
Acquisition Premium	This is the premium over the market value investors have to pay in order to reach control of the target. For non public companies, this value should be zero; for public companies, this value varies according to industry and market conditions, often in the range from 10% to 50%.
Minimum equity in % of acquisition price	In case the debt capacity for new debt is more than 90% of the acquisition price (i.e. the deal can be fully or nearly financed only by debt), this number indicates the required minimum participation of equity holders in the acquisition. This is in fact a rare and special case only for companies with very low valuations and substantial debt capacity. The minimum equity participation assures that these companies can be considered in the model with realistic assumptions.
Exit EV/EBIT when EV at base year < 0	For companies with negative enterprise values, the exit EV/EBIT multiple has to estimated as it cannot be derived from the acquisition multiple. Therefore, this number is the assumed multiple at the time of the exit at which the company will be valued.

Appendix B: Excel Instructions

General Please make sure file name is Technology Buyouts.xls. If file name is changed, [Technology Buyouts.xls] must be replaced on all sheets with [new_filename.xls] When opening the spread sheet, please click 'no' if asked to update linked data. When asked whether to allow macros while opening the spread sheet, click 'yes'.

Macro / IRR The macro will take all companies through the LBO model and store the IRR for each company in the ScreeningData sheet (from which they are automatically applied to all other sheets). To use the macro, click on the 'tools' menu, then click 'macro', then click 'macros...'. Select the macro named 'Main' and click run. WARNING: THE MACRO WILL RUN FOR SEVERAL MINUTES. DURING THAT TIME EXCEL WILL NOT RESPOND. So be prepared to wait or work with another program during that time. You can also have the InputsLBO sheet open before you start the macro, and see Excel pull all data through that sheet.

Ranking To rank the results, to go the Ranking sheet and use the sort function. Further instruction on the sheet.

Individual Analysis To analyze individual companies, enter their data in the orange Bloomberg fields of the InputsLBO sheet.

Adjusting The main two sheets for adjusting the model and altering the results according to your own specifics are the ScoringInputs sheet, where you can change the scale and weight of every parameter used for the attractiveness evaluation, and the InputsLBO sheet, where you can change the assumptions of the LBO model. All changes made in the ScoringInputs sheet will immediately update all results. Changes made to the LBO model in the InputsLBO sheet will only be effective for all companies once the macro has run.

Updating Company Data To update financial data of the companies using the Bloomberg API for Excel, first delete all data fields in the Bloomberg sheet (excluding the field name row on the top and the Bloomberg ticker column on the left). Then place the mouse on top of the ticker column and on the left of the row containing the Bloomberg field names. Following this, apply the "Fill Range" function of the Bloomberg Add-in, and all data will be updated. Note that the currency of all data needs to be consistent. If some data is in other currencies, these need to be converted. Also, make sure the punctuation settings of your system are in sync with those of the Bloomberg data. If you would like to update data using other information systems, you need to completely replace the company list of Bloomberg. See Adding/Replacing Companies.

Adding/ Replacing Companies To add or replace companies in bulk, the Excel API of the respective information systems should be used. (If only the IRR for one specific company is needed, it is much faster to enter the company information into the InputsLBO sheet directly). First, you need to find the ticker symbols for each company of your utilized information system. If you use Bloomberg, a simple way would be to run the bulk wizard in a separate workbook and list all members of an index that you would like to analyze. Note that before you can paste the ticker symbols into the Bloomberg sheet, you must add "equity" behind each symbol (automated when using the replace function). Then you can paste all new ticker symbols over the existing ticker symbols in the Bloomberg sheet and delete the rest. Finally, use the "Fill Range" function as described in Updating Company Data and all new companies are now included in the model. Before you can compare the results, run the macro to get each company's IRR. In case other information systems are used, additionally to pasting new ticker symbols, you must also update the field name row at the top of the Bloomberg sheet. E.g. you need to replace the Bloomberg field name "Cur Mkt Cap" for current market capitalization with the corresponding field name of the system that you use. Finally, apply an equivalent function to fill the table.